THE POWER IN A NAME

A TREASURE MAP TO YOUR IDENTITY AND A ROAD MAP TO YOUR DESTINY

Bethany Hicks and Dan McCollam

Copyright © 2023 by Bethany Hicks and Dan McCollam

All rights reserved.

No portion of this book may be reproduced in any form without written permission from the publisher or author, except as permitted by U.S. copyright law.

All Scripture quotations, unless otherwise indicated, are taken from the Holy Bible, New International Version®, NIV®. Copyright ©1973, 1978, 1984, 2011 by Biblica, Inc.™ Used by permission of Zondervan. All rights reserved worldwide. www.zondervan.com The "NIV" and "New International Version" are trademarks registered in the United States Patent and Trademark Office by Biblica, Inc.™

Some Scripture quotations may be from *The Message*. Copyright © 1993, 1994, 1995, 1996, 2000, 2001, 2002. Used by permission of NavPress Publishing Group.

Some Scripture quotations may be from the NEW AMERICAN STANDARD BIBLE®, Copyright © 1960,1962,1963,1968,1971,1972,1973,1975,1977,1995 by The Lockman Foundation. Used by permission.

Some Scripture quotations may be from *Holy Bible*, New Living Translation, copyright © 1996, 2004, 2015 by Tyndale House Foundation. Used by permission of Tyndale House Publishers, Inc., Carol Stream, Illinois 60188. All rights reserved.

Some Scripture quotations may be from The ESV® Bible (The Holy Bible, English Standard Version®), copyright © 2001 by Crossway, a publishing ministry of Good News Publishers. Used by permission. All rights reserved.

Cover art by The Cloud Digital at 99designs.com.

Published by Prophetic Company, Inc., PO Box 7216, Round Rock, TX 78683

ISBN: 978-0-9851863-9-5

Contents

Introduction	1
1. What's in a Name?	3
2. Internal Boxes That Define You	17
3. External Boxes That Define You	31
4. Scripture Reveals Your Last Name	49
5. Prophecy Reveals Your First Name	59
6. The Meaning of Your Name	71
7. Name Associations	85
8. Name Wordplays	97
9. Names of Places	107
10. Called by a New Name	117
11. Your Heavenly Identity Statement	127
12. Owning Your Name	137
13. Warring with Your Name	145
14. Living from Heavenly Authority	157
15. Heavenly Identity Shapes Culture	167
16. Name Above All Names	177

About the Authors 187

Resources 189

Introduction

You don't need prophetic insight to see the prevailing identity crisis of our time. While it's widely recognized that having a strong sense of self is crucial for living a fulfilling, liberated, and healthy life, there remains some uncertainty in the journey of self-discovery. Countless self-help books, life coaches, and contemporary leaders offer valuable guidance on understanding your current self. However, we contend that most of these resources focus solely on discovering your earthly self but are rarely effective in discovering your heavenly self.

Your heavenly identity is your truest self—the person you were created to be, the highest and most complete version of yourself. Discovering your heavenly identity is only possible when you invite God into the equation of your identity. After all, the One who designed you knows you best.

At the end of the day, we are all creations, and by definition, a creation necessitates a creator. In the case of humankind, we are created in the image of our Creator. Therefore, it is in Him alone that we discover our truest selves and find meaning.

Even if you currently believe and agree that your heavenly identity is crucial to your destiny, the next question you must ask is, "How do I discover my unique identity as defined by God?" If His words about you hold the most potent truth regarding your identity, what are the practical methods through which you can uncover who He says you are? Furthermore, how can you effectively live from your truest self to see the fulfillment of your purpose and God-given destiny? This is where *The Power in a Name* comes in.

In the forthcoming chapters, our aim is to provide you with powerful and biblical tools that will assist you in discovering who God says you are, using the redemptive and prophetic lens of your name. Personally, we have experienced life-changing transformations through this practice. Moreover, we have witnessed its profound impact on countless believers over the past several decades.

In addition to the personal impact, we firmly believe that the tools presented in this book will empower you to become a carrier and catalyst of heavenly identity to a world that is longing to discover its truest self. The Lord is seeking individuals who are willing to bridge the gap between what Heaven declares and what the enemy attempts to distort.

Our prayer is that as you delve into the pages of this book, you embark on a journey. May you uncover the treasures hidden within the wonderful names by which He calls you. As you embrace your true identity, may you confidently and wholeheartedly navigate the roadmap that leads to your God-given destiny.

Chapter 1

What's in a Name?

What if we told you that the answers to two of life's greatest questions—"Who am I?" and "Why am I alive?"—can be found in your name? This book is a compass guiding you on a discovery of the practical and spiritual insights that a name holds. By understanding the power in a name, you will not only possess the ability to chart the course of your own God-given journey but also unlock those hidden secrets for others and the world around you. Think of your name as a treasure map leading you to your unique identity and as a road map guiding you toward the fulfillment of your destiny.

To read this map correctly, one must first understand why a name is so powerful. Everyone has a name; it's common to all humanity. Naming something or someone is to acknowledge its existence as separate from every other thing in the universe. Your name sets you apart as a unique identifier. This is true not only for people but also for all things in our universe. Every discovery, whether a microscopic particle or a massive galaxy system, must be named to give it a sense of separateness and unique existence.

However, your name is more than merely an identifier. While names set us apart, they also help us to understand our connection and belonging within a greater category. You exist and interact within a larger framework of named things. For example, each species of animal or plant has a unique name to differentiate it from other species, which helps scientists study and understand the common characteristics and behaviors of beings belonging within each species. For instance, let's say you looked out the window one day and saw two birds. One is called a Blue Jay, and the other is called a Cardinal. Though they both belong to the broader category of birds, they are also unique and distinct from each other. These names help us understand that they are different types of birds. The study of these relationships and interactions is an essential part of understanding the natural world and our place in it.

In the same way, each of our names, while distinctive, connects us to our families, cultures, and even history. Names are like special links that tie us to certain ideas, people, and places. For example, let's say your name is Lily. The name Lily might remind you of a beautiful flower that your parents had an affinity for, or perhaps it's a name that has been passed down through generations in your family. Whatever the reason, your name tells a story about your connections, and those connections relate to a specific purpose or function.

> "Names are both a treasure map and a road map."

Your name then reveals the perfect paradox of your uniqueness and your connectedness, your identity and your destiny, who you are and how you relate and contribute to the world around you. Names are both a treasure map and a road map. The uniqueness of your name speaks to the timeless question "Who Am I?" and your connectedness speaks to your need to understand your function and why you exist.

NAMES IN CREATION

The ancient writings of the Bible illustrate the power of a name from its very first chapters. God named everything He had made. In the beginning, when God created light and separated the light from the darkness, He named them *day* and *night* respectively. He defined the expanse of the heavens by calling it *sky*, and the dry ground He called *land*. As the Master Creator gathered the waters together, He named them *seas*.

God's naming what He created infers that the act of naming is essential to the existence of all things, providing identity and purpose. Nothing exists that does not have a name, and that name speaks to the core and essential nature of the thing named. In fact, the importance of this process of naming can be seen in that after God created Adam, He delegated the responsibility and authority of naming the creatures to Adam.

NAMES IN ANCIENT CULTURE

From creation forward, the power of a name is evident throughout the holy writ. The people within its pages seemed to understand that a person's name provided insight into their nature. For example, the name *Jacob* means *supplanter* or *heel holder*. A supplanter is defined as one who *takes the place of another, as through force, scheming, or strategy*.[1] When Jacob twice supplants his brother Esau by stealing his blessing and birthright, Esau responded, "Is he not rightly named Jacob?"[2] Esau grasped that Jacob's name as *one who strategizes to take the place of another* was related to the nature of who he was and how he might behave.

In another example, we find the wise young woman Abigail intercepting the wrath of David on behalf of her foolish husband Nabal. She begs David to ignore the wickedness of her husband by saying, "He is just like his name – His name means Fool, and folly goes with him."[3]

Though neither of these illustrations sounds much like a treasure map, they both emphasize that biblical characters believed the roadmap principle that a person's name was linked to their nature. We are in no way saying that the negative connotation of a name guarantees bad behavior as though mankind has no choice in the matter. Rather, our goal is to pull out the highest treasures of our names so that we might conform to their full potential.

To further illustrate the positive connection of a name and its influence on a person's nature, we've compiled the following short sample list of names from the Bible and how they directly shaped the nature and purpose of the person bearing the name.

- Eve - *Life or Living*. Eve was so named because she was to become the mother of all the living.

- Moses - *Pull or Draw Out*. Moses was drawn out of the Nile River as a baby by Pharaoh's daughter, and he was also God's deliverer to draw the Israelites out of slavery into freedom.

- Esther - *Star*. Esther's inner and outer beauty allowed her to outshine the other candidates and win the heart of the king, which later enabled her to save her people.

- David - *Beloved*. David is forever known as a *man after God's heart*[4] whose passion for God forever outweighed his mistakes.

- Barnabas - *Son of Encouragement*. Barnabas' role in supporting and encouraging both Paul and John Mark were essential to the development and growth of the early church.

> "Your name is your calling card, announcing the treasure of your nature."

Each of the names above is interwoven into the identities and destinies of these biblical characters, and the same is true for us. Your name is your calling card, announcing the treasure of your nature. It tells others who you are and how they can relate to you. Understanding this powerful connection is why the names we are called should be carefully considered, allowing only the redemptive lens of who God says we are to pass through our filter of agreement.

NAMES IN MODERN CULTURE

The power of a name seems to be intuitively understood within modern culture. Parents often dream years in advance or agonize for months over what they will name their children. It is a sobering task to think that the name you choose for someone will be an identifier for them for the rest of their life.

However, if your parents did not fully understand the significance of the name they chose for you, there are still great treasures to be found within it.

MARAH *(Dano)*

I once experienced a remarkable example of how God sees a name that may otherwise carry a potentially negative meaning.

Marah never liked her name. When I first met her, she was serving some of the speakers at the conference I was attending. Her jet-black hair hung to her chin in a short crop that often concealed her eyes. It did not take great prophetic insight to interpret her slumping posture and unkempt appearance: Marah had identity issues. Making friendly eye contact with her, I greeted Marah and asked her if she knew what her name meant. Marah glanced down at the carpet and replied, "Yes. It means bitter."

The name Marah is related to a Bible story in chapter fifteen of the Book of Exodus. In this account, the thirsty, traveling Israelites came upon a place called Marah, but they could not drink the water there because it was bitter. God told Moses to throw a certain branch into the bitter water, and the water miraculously became fit to drink.

I caught her eyes again and said, "Marah, you're not the bitter waters. You are the place where bitter waters become sweet." Her countenance dawned with a bit of hope as I continued, "I believe God has given you a ministry of reconciliation. You carry the ability to help people who are bitter of heart or in bitter circumstances to recognize the presence of the Branch, Jesus. You are meant to bring sweetness and life. That is what your name means."

Marah's eyes spilled over with tears. "I have never liked my name. I've even thought about legally changing it."

"But not now," I interjected. She smiled widely and shook her head. "Not now," she agreed.

God knew you before the foundation of the world, and He has woven into the fabric of your being the treasure that He created you to be. He has embedded a significant potential destiny within the power of your name. Even if your name comes with a negative meaning or connotation, the Redeemer of all things has a redemptive identity and purpose for you. God's view of your name has the power to supersede and restore everything to who and what you were created to be.

NAMES REVEAL AUTHORITY AND RESPONSIBILITY

The power in your name can also be affirmed in the Bible's definition of the word *name*. The Greek word translated *name* in the New Testament is *onoma* which is described this way: *The name is used for everything which the name covers. Everything, the thought or feeling of which is aroused in the mind by mentioning, hearing, remembering, the name.*[5] The point is that every name holds within it a sense of identification, authority, and responsibility for everything that is associated with that name.

The power of names, therefore, not only links individuals to their identity and nature but also reveals the authority and responsibility that is inherently attached to them. For example, when your kids call you *Mom* or *Dad*, those names are so much more than identifiers for your children. Those labels carry significant weight, representing the authority and responsibility that you hold in your children's lives as their parent. As their mom or dad, you carry unique authority to speak into the lives of those you love and care for. You are responsible for nurturing, protecting, providing, and raising them to be the world-changers God says they are. No one else holds that role in your children's lives while you are alive on this earth, except in cases where one forfeits that authority and responsibility to someone else through inability, negligence, or abuse. This irreplaceable role and all that it entails is summed up in the names *Mom* and *Dad*.

NURSE LYNELL *(Bethany)*

My mother was a registered nurse and served in a variety of healthcare fields. She was Nurse Lynell for over 40 years. I remember one instance when I was a teenager where our family was eating at a restaurant. Suddenly, a man at another table started choking, and his face began to turn purple. As quick as a flash, my mom ran to this gentleman, turned him around, and performed the Heimlich maneuver on him, thus dislodging the food particle stuck in his throat so he could breathe again. My mother did not hesitate to jump into action because she understood her name. As *nurse*, she was aware of all the responsibilities associated with that name and embraced the authority that came with it as well, even when she was "off the clock." When you know your name, you understand your authority.

THE AUTHORITY OF GOD'S NAMES

The Bible mentions more than 967 names and titles referring to the one true God, each revealing an aspect of His nature and character.[6] For example, the name Jehovah-Jireh means t*he Lord will provide.*[7] This name reveals God's authority as the source of all provision and His declaration of responsibility that He will supply our needs according to His riches in glory. Another name He reveals of Himself is Jehovah-Rapha which means *the Lord who heals.*[8] This name conveys God's authority to heal and His responsibility to restore us to health.

In the New Testament, Jesus is referred to as Emmanuel which means *God with us.*[9] This name speaks to His authority as God in human form and His responsibility to be present with us always.

As we explore the names of God in the Bible, we come to understand that God is not a distant deity but is intimately involved in every aspect of our lives. His names communicate His authority and responsibility to care for us, provide for us, heal us, guide us, and so much more.

The first recorded instance in scripture where God personally revealed His name is found in the Book of Exodus during an exchange with Moses. God appeared to Moses in a burning bush and informed him that He had called him to deliver His people Israel out of Egypt. Interestingly, Moses did not directly ask God how He would accomplish this mighty deed but instead asked for the name he should give the Israelite leaders when they asked who sent him.

> Moses said to God, "Suppose I go to the Israelites and say to them, 'The God of your fathers has sent me to you,' and they ask me, 'What is his name?' Then what shall I tell them?" God said to Moses, "I am who I am. This is what you are to say to the Israelites: 'I AM has sent me to you.'" God also said to Moses, "Say to the Israelites, 'The LORD the God of your fathers — the God of Abraham, the God of Isaac and the God of Jacob — has sent me to you.' This is my name forever, the name you shall call me from generation to generation."
>
> Exodus 3:13-15

This may seem like a small detail, but it was quite significant for Moses to know the name of the One sending him. He needed to have the authority and backing of God to convince the Israelite elders and the entire population of Hebrews to follow him. Without this name, he would have been just another person claiming to have a plan for their deliverance.

God understood Moses' need for this validation and responded by revealing His primary name: I AM. This name is powerful and significant because it declares God's eternal existence and self-sufficiency. By revealing His name to Moses, God was establishing His authority and presence as the One sending him. This name and all that it entailed gave Moses the confidence and backing he needed to approach the Israelite leaders with the message of their deliverance.

RENAME TO REDEFINE

The power and nature of a name is not lost to the enemy of all mankind either. Currently, there seems to be a cultural trend to rename or redefine certain things away from God's original design. As an example, there have been attempts by some political leaders in the United States to rename *woman* as *menstruating person* and *mother* as *birthing person*. This renaming is more than simple semantics or a preference of language; it's an attempt to redefine the nature of women and mothers away from who and what God created them to be. It's a tragic repetition of an age-old story where created beings position themselves as superior to their Creator and attempt to fix His "mistakes." Renaming is like trying to erase a part of who we were created to be. It can disconnect us from God's original blueprint for our lives, potentially causing great harm to our core sense of self. To avoid false narratives, we should never live from names that contradict what God says or has said about us.

You might be recalling biblical instances where God renamed people and places and are wondering what is so wrong with renaming if God did it? When God assigned a new name, it was an upgrade of identity connected to the release of a new season and destiny. It was an addition to the receiver's identity rather than a replacement. When God gives a new name, it's always to bring us into a higher view and heavenly perspective not lesser. In Him, we go from glory to glory and from strength to strength. The new name is not a downgrade of the essential nature or core identity of the original name. In fact, when we discover all the names God gives us, they come together like building blocks, enhancing the fullness of our heavenly identity.

YOUR HEAVENLY IDENTITY

Renaming is not the only challenge to the power in a name. We need to make sure we are embracing the correct and redemptive lens of who God says we are. Like Marah in our story, we must reject any inferior or lesser identity attached to our name and view ourselves according to how God defines us. Seeing ourselves or others as God does is what we call understanding heavenly identity. The names that God calls us reveal the seeds of our heavenly identity that will propel us into the highest and best version of ourselves, the truest self we were created to be.

The naming pattern in creation, the writings of the Bible, the emphasis on names within modern culture, and the names of God Himself all show that a person's name is deeply woven into their identity and destiny. Each name holds a treasure map revealing the truest version of ourselves and a roadmap of purpose, authority, and responsibility. Since destiny flows from identity, it's crucial to identify and reject any inferior names that have been assigned to us so we can embrace the truth of our heavenly identities and fulfill our purposes.

In the upcoming chapters, we will identify the sources of false identities and inferior name definitions that you may have been living under. After exposing the lies of any false names, we will offer practical tools for understanding the spiritual significance of names, helping you discover who God says you truly are and how it relates to your God-given purpose on Earth. Lastly, you will learn to wield the power of your name like a sword, cutting away lies and hindrances, so you can step into the fullness of your world-changing destiny.

CHAPTER REFLECTIONS

Do you like or identify with your name? Why or why not?

_____

_____

_____

_____

Describe a person you know whose name doesn't fit who they are. Why don't you think their name fits them?

_____

_____

_____

_____

Jesus asked his disciples, "Who do you say that I am?" What name best describes God for you in your current season and why?

_____

_____

_____

_____

CHAPTER END NOTES

1. Dictionary.com.

2. Genesis 27:36.

3. 1 Samuel 25:25.

4. Acts 13:22.

5. Accessed May 18, 2023.

6. https://christiananswers.net/dictionary/namesofgod.html. Accessed July 13, 2023.

7. Genesis 22:14.

8. Exodus 15:26.

9. Matthew 1:23.

Chapter 2

Internal Boxes That Define You

Our given names are not the only names we live by. Many of us have taken on false names and fake IDs shaped by wrong ideas of who we truly are. Before you can move forward in discovering the treasures of your identity, you need to shed these hindrances from your journey thus far. The greatest obstacle to moving forward in your calling and purpose is not your education, gifting, opportunities, qualifications, age, or gender. While all these factors certainly contribute to your identity, at the end of the day, the primary obstacle to your mobilization into destiny is what you have believed about yourself—the false names *you* believe in, the inferior names *you* accept—and how those have shaped your mindsets.

To discover your true identity, it is essential to identify and reject any false names you may have come into agreement with. Breaking these false identity barriers allows you to embrace the truth of who Heaven says you are. These inferior names collectively shape the "boxes" in your life that constrain you.

A box is something meant to contain or limit. Metaphorically, boxes represent anything that is attempting to hinder you from being all that God says you are. Internal boxes refer to the mindsets, beliefs, and thoughts we have about ourselves. These are the false names or deceitful definitions that we have come to believe about ourselves internally which we are consciously or unconsciously living by. Every name, true or false, with which you associate yourself has the potential to shape your identity and establish your destiny.

THE SOURCE OF OUR INTERNAL BOXES

Where did these wrong ideas about who we are come from? False mindsets and beliefs could have been introduced by any number of sources, e.g., a family member, a book, other children at school, a movie or television show, or even a demonically introduced thought. The key to note here is that the internal thoughts, belief systems, or false names that negatively define you were something you knowingly or unconsciously agreed with. Agreement is what gives a name power. If you are struggling under the influence of a false name, at some point in your life, there was a form of agreement that allowed that false name to shape your identity.

We likely all have internal boxes formed by untrue names, some of which we may not even be consciously aware of. For example, many individuals believe that no one truly knows them except for themselves. While the individual may be completely convinced, this deception leaves God's voice out of the equation. Having a right view of ourselves is a rare commodity.

> "Agreement is what gives a name power."

Even some of the Bible's greatest heroes had wrong ideas about themselves that worked at limiting their effectiveness.

MOSES THE DELIVERER

Out of the multitude of Hebrews living in Egypt in the 13th century BC, Moses was uniquely qualified for his future destiny. Moses was living as a free man in a palace while his own people suffered as slaves of Egypt, laboring under extremely harsh conditions. When the Lord heard the cries of His people and looked for a deliverer, Moses was the clear and obvious candidate. Why? Because God needed someone with a free mindset to lead His people out of slavery into freedom. You can't bring another person into freedom and breakthrough if you're bound by the same things they are. Albert Einstein is reported to have said, "You cannot solve a problem with the same mindset that created it." It takes a free person to set others free.

In the Book of Exodus when the Lord approached Moses and called him to bring the Israelites out of Egypt, Moses had an issue with himself. There was a snag in the fabric of his perspective. To understand Moses' internal box, let's take a closer look at his response to the Lord's call:

> Moses said to the Lord, "Pardon your servant, Lord. I have never been eloquent, neither in the past nor since you have spoken to your servant. I am slow of speech and tongue."
>
> Exodus 3:10

Moses, a prince of Egypt who was exposed to the highest education and arts of his time, experienced an internal identity crisis. Despite his royal upbringing, he didn't believe he could be who God was calling him to be. It appears that Moses believed he needed eloquence of speech to confront Pharaoh and lead Israel out of slavery. He felt that his lack of effective communication skills disqualified him as a deliverer.

Moses had placed an internal box on his identity by naming himself as a poor public speaker. Some theologians say that Moses stuttered; others think he simply had a fear of public speaking. If the latter were true, Moses would not stand alone in this. Researchers suggest that glossophobia, a fear of public speaking, is a very common dread affecting up to 75% of the earth's population.

Fears and feelings of inadequacy are among the thoughts that restrict us and prevent us from embracing our truest identity and fulfilling our God-given purposes. When we label ourselves based on our deficiencies, we create an internal box that confines our identity and restricts our potential to what we believe internally about ourselves. Moses almost missed his destiny because of the limitations of his perceived internal identity.

When Moses was faced with the call of God on his life, he had a decision to make. He viewed himself in one way, but God rightly saw him differently. Which one would he choose? Although the Lord conceded to enlisting the help of his brother Aaron, scripture records a glowing report of how Moses was remembered hundreds of years later. In the Book of Acts, while recounting the history of Israel, Stephen the martyr describes Moses as a man "powerful in speech and action."[1] It appears from the biblical record that at some point, Moses chose to trust the Lord's perspective by rejecting the internal lies and fulfilled his destiny as the great deliverer of Israel.

GRASSHOPPER VISION

A generation later, in another biblical event, we witness an extreme contrast in what two different mindsets can produce even when evaluating the same thing.

When the twelve spies of Israel were commissioned to scout out the promised land of Canaan, they each witnessed and reported that the land was rich and fertile, yielding a harvest of milk, honey, and other crops that were abundant and lavish. They all agreed that the promised land was as great as the Lord had said. Here is where the commonalities end.

Though all twelve spies saw that there were giants in the land that would need to be overtaken, only Joshua and Caleb had the correct lens of who they were as Israelites, called by God as His chosen people. The ten remaining spies had an inferior internal mindset claiming, "We were like grasshoppers in our own eyes."[2]

Rather than looking to the Lord and believing in the truth of God's promise over them, in their hearts, they agreed with the false name of *grasshoppers*. This distorted perception of their internal identity ended up costing an entire generation entrance into the Promised Land. Multiplied thousands died in the desert without living in the fullness of their identity or fulfilling their destiny. Why? Because what you believe about your identity will either promote you into destiny or cause you to forfeit it. Joshua and Caleb, on the other hand, triumphantly crossed into the Promised Land because they rightly saw God as powerful and themselves as able to take the land through Him.

Joshua and Caleb's belief about their identity directly affected what they believed they could do. The same is true for you. None of us can afford to acquiesce to these internal lying names and mindsets any longer.

> "What you believe about your identity will either promote you into destiny or cause you to forfeit it."

THROW OFF WHAT HINDERS

The writer of Hebrews tells us what to do with these boxes that limit, suppress, or immobilize us from advancing in the truth:

> Throw off everything that hinders and the sin that so easily entangles. And let us run with perseverance the race marked out for us....
>
> Hebrews 12:1

It is possible to misinterpret this passage as "throw off every sin that hinders and so easily entangles." However, it is clear that the author of this text was drawing a distinction between sin and other obstacles that hinder us from our destiny. Sin is not the only entanglement; there are other hindrances. According to the Greek definition, a hindrance is something that burdens or weighs you down.[3]

False identities qualify as hindrances. These fake ID "boxes" are crafted by the enemy with the sole purpose of hindering you at best and at worst completely shutting you down from accomplishing your race. False or inaccurate names adopted by you will weigh you down with unnecessary entanglements.

In this passage, the solution to throwing off these needless burdens is clear. You don't need to accommodate the box, tolerate the box, or manage the box. You need to break the box! You have the power in Christ to throw off everything that hinders!

What boxes of self-belief are hindering your race now? It's not always clear. We do not always recognize that we are believing a lie about ourselves. False internal names cloud our perspective and hinder our God-given destiny.

THE LIE OF SHY *(Bethany)*

When my oldest daughter Faith was a toddler, she would run errands with me to various stores to purchase food and supplies for the family. Often, when at a store or coffee shop, I would run into someone I knew in the small mountain town and begin talking with them. I would then introduce my friend to my daughter and say, "Faith, can you say hello to Ms. So-and-so?" to which my lovely daughter would scrunch her face in a defiant way while sharply shaking her head "no" and turning her back.

Now, I'm not the type of parent that demands perfection from my children, but rudeness was not something I would tolerate. Additionally, I recognized that something else was at play here. So, privately when it was just her and me, I would ask Faith what was going on in her heart when those situations would arise. In her little toddler's voice, Faith responded, "I shy, Mommy. I shy."

Her answer troubled me. My fierce and strong daughter had an internal box that was contrary to her nature. She believed that she was shy, which prevented her from engaging with other people. I believe that the name *shy* is a lie from the enemy. You won't find shyness being praised or encouraged anywhere in scripture, and it's certainly not listed as one of the fruits of the Spirit. Neither is shyness a personality type;

but rather, it's an internal box that we can create for ourselves when we believe its lie.

I recognized that this mindset was working its way into my daughter's belief system, and as a result, Faith was beginning to adopt the name *shy* as an identity. This may seem trivial to some, but I have witnessed many of my friends live under the limiting belief of shyness for decades. I've seen how this insidious lie hindered their purpose and calling. As her mother, I was determined not to let my daughter's identity be constrained by this internal label. Her future depended on it!

To counter the lie, I would deposit truth into my daughter and say to her, "Faith, you're not shy. You have the Lion of the Tribe of Judah living inside of you, and He is roaring!" I would reinforce this truth at every opportunity, and after about six months, I noticed a change in Faith. Little by little, when we would be out running errands and would come across friends of mine, Faith would begin to talk with them. She took baby steps out of her false identity and into her heavenly one. Today, nearly fifteen years later, Faith is just like her name–bold, fearless and by far, the most outgoing and sociable of my children.

If you are reading this now and have identified with the lie of shy in the past, we want to encourage you that it's time to break free from that crippling internal identity and step into the boldness and confidence that God has for you. Shy is no longer your name!

Grasshoppers, shy, not eloquent enough—these lies may not seem all that powerful, but names and titles can have a huge impact on our lives. If we believe and internalize them, they have the potential to hinder our destiny in a significant way. Let's look at another internal box that hinders our running the race.

REGRETS AND FAILURES

Past mistakes can become an internal box if we allow them to define our identity. Peter, Jesus' most outspoken disciple, had to deal with his own identity crises as one who disowned Jesus in His darkest hour. In the hours leading to Jesus' crucifixion and resurrection, Peter denied knowing Jesus three times. Scripture records that on the third time, Jesus turned and looked directly at Peter. That look from the suffering Savior and his own sense of personal failure must have cut him to the core of his being because Peter wept bitterly.[4]

After Jesus had risen from the dead, Peter returned to fishing. Perhaps the former fisherman thought himself now disqualified from his higher call and therefore returned to the comfortable and familiar. But the risen Jesus wasn't about to let Peter live hindered by that internal perception, so he confronted Peter on the shore of the lake. Let's look in on the story in the writing of John the disciple.

> When they had finished eating, Jesus said to Simon Peter, "Simon son of John, do you truly love me more than these?" "Yes, Lord," he said, "you know that I love you." Jesus said, "Feed my lambs." Again, Jesus said, "Simon son of John, do you truly love me?" He answered, "Yes, Lord, you know that I love you." Jesus said, "Take care of my sheep." The third time he said to him, "Simon son of John, do you love me?"

> Peter was hurt because Jesus asked him the third time, "Do you love me?" He said, "Lord, you know all things; you know that I love you." Jesus said, "Feed my sheep."
>
> John 21:15-17

How did Jesus break Peter's internal lens of failure and feelings of disqualification? The first thing Jesus did was to correct Peter's identity. He challenged Peter to remember and reassess his love for God, but He also confirmed Peter's purpose as one who would care for His sheep. Jesus shifted Peter's self-perception. Was the former fisherman a faithless denier who had rendered himself unworthy and disqualified? Or was he the loving follower of Jesus who would help build God's unshakable kingdom? Was Peter still worthy to lead and feed the sheep?

It is important to understand that Simon Peter's identity and calling from the Lord were never based on his previous gifts or performance. Remember, Peter wasn't necessarily worthy or qualified when the Lord had originally called him as a young fisherman. The disciple had to choose again whether he would agree with God's heavenly view of him or settle for a lesser earthly identity. All of us must do the same.

DO NOT BENCH YOURSELF

In sports, the bench is where team players sit who are not currently participating in the game. Some of those on the bench may be less skilled players waiting for an opportunity to relieve the first-string players; but some may be sitting on the bench as a form of penalty or discipline. The benched players must watch others do what they have trained to do. The point here is don't bench yourself! It's easy to come under the name "disqualified" due to past wrong choices, behaviors, or decisions that cause us to effectively bench ourselves from running our own race. Obviously, we all make mistakes, and it is important to repent and clean up our messes.

However, your past mistakes should not define who you are. A mistake is something you do, not who you are. Even identity shaped by chronic failures or false mindsets can be realigned when submitted to the truth of who God says you are.

There is a vast difference between a single misbehavior and your truest identity. Telling a single lie does not redefine you as a liar. Peter denied the Lord, but he was not inherently a coward. His short season of failure did not represent the totality of his being; it was a fear he gave in to in the moment. Simon Peter had a heavenly identity and destiny as a builder of Christ's church against whom the gates of hell would not prevail. Yet, as Peter stood before Jesus, he was presented with a choice: Would the disciple live from his truest identity as one who loves the Lord and feeds His sheep, or would he choose to align with the false name of *disqualified*?

We all have a heavenly identity and God-given destiny that is infinitely greater than the sum of our failures. This truth is a liberating revelation that is desperately needed today. Countless lives are functioning from a false identity based upon something they did wrong yesterday. It is time to throw off those internal belief systems and untrue names that have been holding you back.

Regardless of your circumstance, Jesus paid too high of a price for you to live from anything less than who He says you are. His death, resurrection, and ascension are your assurance that you can put to death those internal lies and behaviors that have been shaping your self-view. Don't live from a lesser perspective of yourself than He has of you. Nothing you can do will change who He says you are. But what you believe about what He says will determine whether it will be seen on the earth or not. Your journey is about discovering, believing, and living out the truth of what God is speaking over your identity.

Ask the Holy Spirit to search you with the candle of His goodness to reveal any internal hindrances to your journey. You might also inquire of a trusted friend or leader to share if they have seen things you believe about yourself that have formed boxes of limitations. When revealed, none of these things need hinder you. Break those internal boxes and embrace the true you in Christ Jesus. In the chapters ahead, we will give you tools to recalibrate your perspective to see as He sees because the truest thing about you in the universe is who God says you are.

CHAPTER REFLECTIONS

What past failures, lies, or false identities have most hindered you from running?

_____

_____

_____

_____

Bethany tells the story of how she released her daughter from the lie of being shy by reminding her that the Lion of Judah lived within her. Do you know any friends or family members who are living under an inferior identity? What could you say or do to help them break free from that box?

_____

_____

_____

_____

A wrong internal view of God can also limit your ability to access His goodness. Believing that God always wants to punish you, find fault with you, or reject you are internal lies that must be broken. Can you describe a time when you had an inferior view of God that limited your ability to relate to Him? Ask the Holy Spirit to reveal any current views you hold of God that don't measure up to His goodness.

CHAPTER END NOTES

1. Acts 7:22.

2. Numbers 13:33.

3. "G3591 - ogkos - Strong's Greek Lexicon (niv)." No Pages. Cited 22 May 2023. https://www.blueletterbible.org/lexicon/g3591/niv/mgnt/0-1/.

4. Matthew 26:75.

Chapter 3

External Boxes That Define You

The internal lies you have believed are not the only obstacles that can hinder your identity and destiny. Many of us are also constrained by external boxes that seek to define and restrict who we are and what we are capable of. These external constraints are created by the influence of others or by circumstances that impose certain identities upon us, sometimes even successfully. While internal boxes are associated with the inner realm of mindsets and beliefs, external boxes are formed outside of us by factors such as other people's expectations, peer opinions, societal traditions, and even our own family history. Once again, let's turn to the Bible to discover how Heaven's heroes broke their external boxes in order to live in the fullness of their heavenly identities.

GIDEON, GOD'S MIGHTY WARRIOR

Gideon, the ancient judge of Israel, was not always the powerful deliverer we remember today. In fact, when the Angel of the Lord approached him with the message and assignment to become Israel's champion by overcoming her oppressors, Gideon had an issue with his qualifications. He had an external box shaped by the dictates of his personal status and environment.

> "Pardon me, my lord," Gideon replied, "but how can I save Israel? My clan is the weakest in Manasseh, and I am the least in my family."
>
> Judges 6:15

Gideon was defining his potential by his external circumstances. He disassociated himself from the assignment the Lord was giving him because of the weak position of his lineage and his own placement within the family. I'm the smallest…the weakest…too insignificant to do great things. This dialogue with the angel is more than Gideon's external processing. Through his reply to the angel, he revealed the names he had come into agreement with: *smallest, weakest, insignificant, conquered, victim.*

How many times do we find ourselves in the same situation? We often feel unqualified to participate in the race that God has called us to because we believe that certain external aspects of our identity such as gender, ethnicity, or family background (which are all beyond our control) indicate that we lack what it takes to succeed. Biblically and historically, it appears the Lord takes a certain measure of pleasure in choosing the foolish things of the world to confound the wise.[1]

We see this conflict between Gideon's external reality and his heavenly calling in the Angel of the Lord's initial contact with him. The angel greeted Gideon with the words, "The Lord is with you, mighty warrior."[2] Notice that this greeting was more than mere words. It was a declaration of Gideon's heavenly identity. The Lord proclaimed that He saw Gideon as a mighty warrior. Ironically, at that very moment, Gideon was hiding in a winepress while he threshed wheat because of the intense oppression of Israel's enemies. He certainly did not look like a mighty warrior.

Israel was a conquered country under the hand of yet another oppressive regime. As far as we know, Gideon had never fought a battle or even owned a sword, yet the Lord saw him as a mighty warrior even when he was hiding out! How could Heaven's statement be true when everything around him was screaming an opposite reality? It was a matter of which reality Gideon allowed to define his name.

THE BOTTOM OF THE FOOD CHAIN

Gideon saw himself at the bottom of the proverbial food chain, and yet, the Lord declared him a mighty warrior. Not was or will be but is a mighty warrior. There is a Kingdom truth here that applies to us the same as it did to Gideon. In the earth realm, you are defined by what you do; but in the heavenly realm, you do from who God says you are. You are not a mighty warrior because you have won battles or have proven yourself skilled with a sword. It is because the Lord calls you mighty warrior that you will win battles. Heaven always sees us better than we see ourselves. Heaven sees who we were created to be in Christ Jesus from the foundations of the world. Our journey is to discover, believe, and to walk in the fullness of our heavenly identity just as Gideon learned to do.

> "Heaven always sees us better than we see ourselves."

Interestingly, the truth of Gideon's God-given identity can also be found in the root meaning of his name. Gideon's name means *to cut down, feller, to destroy anything, warrior.* When the Angel of the Lord declared that Gideon was a powerful warrior, he wasn't declaring a new identity to Gideon; He was reminding Gideon of who he was already created to be. The angel was prophesying through the meaning of his name that Gideon was a mighty warrior who was created to cut down and destroy the enemies of Israel. Gideon could have missed his life-changing destiny if he continued to live from the false identity and names related to his outward circumstances. Your history is not the prophet of your destiny. Your environment or lineage cannot limit your God-given potential. Which realm will you let name and define you?

STEPHANIE, TIFFANY, BETHANY *(Bethany)*

Many years ago, we were ministering in a foreign country in a large church. Dano was the main speaker, and I was part of the team that was invited to minister with him. With multiple services seating over a thousand people each, the leaders of this church wanted to honor the team that accompanied Dano. So, before introducing Dano as the speaker, they would announce the name of each team member and that team member's function. When they got to me, they introduced me saying, "This is Dano's assistant Stephanie." The congregation welcomed me with their applause and smiled kindly at me. However, I was not his assistant, and my name was not Stephanie. So in between services, knowing that they would be introducing the team again in the next service, we let the local leader know that my name was Bethany and I worked with Dano not for him. The leaders graciously apologized and assured us that they would correct the information.

So, when the second service rolled around, everything was going well up until my introduction, "*A*nd this is Dano's intern, Tiffany." Now it was getting comical. In the first service I was his assistant Stephanie, and now I was his intern Tiffany. When Dano got up to speak, he graciously clarified who I was for the audience—that my name was Bethany, and I was a pastor at our local church who worked with the mission organization Sounds of the Nations. Once the congregation and leaders saw and identified me rightly, they treated me differently. They began to pull on my grace as a leader and pastor because they understood my correct name.

I share all this not because I was offended; I thought it was hilarious! At the same time, I was not going to identify with a name or position that did not reflect who I truly was. I knew that who God said I am was bigger than their box, and I was not going to let those false labels limit me due to misinformation.

DAVID AND HIS BROTHERS

David, the great psalmist, warrior, and king had his own external boxes to break. Before he became Israel's hero fighting Goliath, he had to fight off the jealous opinions of his older brothers.

> When Eliab, David's oldest brother, heard him speaking with the men, he burned with anger at him and asked, "Why have you come down here? And with whom did you leave those few sheep in the wilderness? I know how conceited you are and how wicked your heart is; you came down only to watch the battle." "Now what have I done?" said David. "Can't I even speak?" He then turned away to someone else and

brought up the same matter, and the men answered him as before.

I Samuel 17:28-30

David's brothers were offended that the younger brother believed he could take down the giant that they themselves were terrified of. They pulled the "older brother card" on David and condescendingly told him to stick to his chores as a shepherd boy and leave the big stuff to the big boys.

This often happens in a family dynamic. We tease one another by calling each other names that are neither true nor kind. False names spoken by a loved one or one in authority have the power to take root and shape a lesser identity if we come into agreement with the lie. When we hear names spoken by people we love or by those who have some level of authority or responsibility in our lives, it can be challenging to discern what is true and what is false. Because of these people's positions in our lives, we believe these lies and think less of ourselves. That is why it is so vital that we all have a personal revelation of who God says we are. When we rightly discern who God made us to be, we can throw off these external identity boxes.

STICKS AND STONES *(Bethany)*

Have you heard the adage, "Sticks and stones may break my bones, but names will never hurt me"? It's a saying that helps children cope with other kids who tease and call them names. The expression implies that one is not affected by taunts or insults. However, when someone is labeled with a derogatory name and it becomes a part of their identity, it hurts.

From the time my children were old enough to talk and fight over toys, I would vigorously interject into any conversation where they assigned a false identity to one another through name calling. Things that we often hear every child say at some point, such as "You're stupid!" or "You're an idiot!" were quickly addressed and corrected because I understood the power of this principle. There is a vast difference between *doing* something stupid and *being* stupid. The former statement is related to a function, while the latter is an assignment of identity. When we repeatedly hear similar statements, especially from those whom our lives are entrusted to, it can be easy to embrace these false names, assume them as our identity, and live according to them.

Years ago, I was ministering at a youth conference where one of the young leaders was sharing how he had recently come out of a homosexual lifestyle. Intrigued, I asked him how he had begun living this lifestyle. He told me that when he was younger, he had a higher voice than was normal for a boy. Other kids would make fun of him and call him a particular derogatory name. This name carried a connotation of homosexuality with it, and since he did not know the truth of his heavenly identity, he eventually adopted this name and thus the lifestyle as his identity. This young man lived in bondage to this external box for thirteen years because he allowed this name calling by other children to define him.

When I was younger, my siblings would tease me by calling me "Breathany" instead of Bethany. It angered me at the time because it implied that I had bad breath.

Years later, as I have pursued my passion to know and understand how Jesus speaks to us through the gift of prophecy, I have come to attach a redemptive meaning to this nickname. In the scriptures, whenever God or Jesus breathed, it was a manifestation of the Holy Spirit's presence. So, I chose to let any haunting remembrance of "Breathany" serve as a reminder that I am filled with the very breath of God, a vessel speaking life everywhere I go.

Over the years of interacting with thousands of people on six continents, I have come to believe that the things you were teased about often represent the enemy's attempts to distort an area of gifting and calling in your life. If this has happened to you, I encourage you to bring that name or label to the Lord and ask Him for His redemptive thoughts to counter what was falsely spoken over you. Let His truth displace every inferior identity and restore you to the way you are known in Heaven.

FAMILIARITY AS A BOX

Jesus, Himself, had to navigate and throw off other people's limited views that did not align with God's purposes. Look at this example recorded by His disciple Matthew:

> Coming to his hometown, he began teaching the people in their synagogue, and they were amazed. "Where did this man get this wisdom and miraculous powers?" they asked. "Isn't this the carpenter's son? Isn't his mother's name Mary, and

aren't his brothers James, Joseph, Simon, and Judas? Aren't all his sisters with us? Where then did this man get all these things?" And they took offense at him.

Matthew 13:54-57

The townspeople of Nazareth associated with Jesus based on their limited knowledge of who He was on earth rather than who Heaven said He was. They named and therefore judged Him based only on His family association and occupation. Since the people would only relate to Jesus on an earthly level, most of them could only receive earthly possibilities. As a result, Jesus could not do many miracles in His hometown. It's a tragedy that an entire town missed out on the beautiful benefits Jesus had to offer because they simply chose not to see past the external box they had placed Him in.

Familiarity can be a limiting external box not only for us but also in how we view others if we allow it to be. Part of this journey of growing into our heavenly identity is making room for others to become who Heaven says they are. This means we must learn to regard no one according to the flesh,[3] or after their earthly performance. Let's practice extending grace to people as they break free from both internal and external limitations and discover who God created them to be.

THE GENDER BOX *(Bethany)*

My primary external box has been my gender and the perceived roles that a woman can operate in within the church. As a woman who is called by God to speak, teach, minister, and lead in the church, it has been challenging at times to fulfill that call while living in a world where these roles have traditionally been filled by men. There were situations when leaders could not see me as the right fit for the job because they were looking for the right *man* not the right *person*.

Even today, I feel the lingering effects of being put in a box when I see conferences with a speaker line-up of three to five men and no women present at the microphone—and it's not even a men's conference! To be clear, I am incredibly thankful for the men who have pioneered the way as teachers, preachers, and conference speakers, and I know that many male leaders in the church are working hard to correct this imbalance. However, we cannot have the full expression of God's voice if half of those created in His image are kept in silence. We are all created to be powerful in Him, and each of us can break the external boxes placed on others by intentionally making room for them. Powerful people make room for others, regardless of gender, age, or race.

THE PERFORMANCE BOX *(Dano)*

I remember a time when I had resigned from my role as worship leader and youth pastor to become an itinerant speaker and missionary. Starting out, invitations were slow to come, so I prayed for opportunities while helping at my local church in my spare time. Being new to self-employment, it took me a while to figure out how to use my time effectively and how to manage my relationships and finances. This position of being somewhat in-between purposes left me feeling undefined. Who am I? A missionary? An itinerant speaker? A church volunteer? I wasn't fully any of those things. Along with the financial pressure of the transition, these questions caused a crisis of identity for me.

Men often feel societal pressure to be the provider for their families. If they are not working or providing, it is easy for them to feel like failures. This internal pressure to work and provide can cause you to name yourself by your profession. In Western culture, we demonstrate this focus on external boxes by introducing ourselves by what we do, such as, "Hi, I'm Steve, and I'm a lawyer" or "I'm Bill, and I'm a teacher." When our title or function is removed or during seasons of transition, men commonly experience a crisis of identity.

It's like the high school football star who is used to receiving honor from his peers. Upon graduation, suddenly his prior identity is no longer relevant. No one sees him with the same honor he had in his previous role, and it can create depression or a desire to perform for identity. When vocation defines you, you relegate identity to something that is somewhat external, subject to change, and, at times, out of your control. That's a dangerous place to live in.

For me, the answer came in dethroning myself as the provider for my family. I still had to be financially responsible and do my part, but ultimately, God is Jehovah Jireh—the One who sees in advance and provides. He sits on the throne of Provider. I had to see that my job was only one stream of God's many strategies for provision. I couldn't let my function define my identity or self-worth. Regardless of my occupation, God saw me as a dearly loved son in whom He delighted. Resting in that place of living from heavenly identity as God's son rather than the function of a ministry or vocational title released the pressure valve of performance and allowed me to live in a more peaceful exploration of my next season.

NAME OF THE MONTH *(Bethany)*

Within the context of external identities, I want to address another disturbing shift concerning names. In modern culture, there is a trend of changing the names or pronouns people identify with. With the rise of self-defining pronouns, it can be challenging to navigate all the different ways people are choosing to identify themselves.

When my youngest daughter attended a public high school, she overheard conversations among other students about changing their names. The current generation often uses the phrase "I identify as..." followed by any word of their choice.

One student in her class found the idea of giving off "vamp" vibes intriguing and decided to change her name and identify as a vampire. And she was not joking. There were other students in my daughter's class who changed their names so frequently that others got confused as to which name to call them.

It's the "name-of-the-month club," and this generation seems to have an unlimited paid subscription. If you no longer like your name, you can change it! If you don't want to be a "he," you can rename yourself as "she" or "they." Multiplied by thousands and thousands of name changes, you eventually have a generational identity crisis.

The purpose of sharing this is not to be a protestor but to emphasize the reality of the power in our names. The name-shifting generation seems to have an intuitive understanding of the influence that a name holds over their identity. When we do not know who God says we are—our truest identity—we either define our own identity or allow others to define it for us. The problem with self-definition is that it can never satisfy the deepest questions that every person on the planet asks: Who am I? What am I made for?

Only the Creator can rightly define His creation. Only a loving God and Father can truly speak to the value of every son and daughter.

CALL ME BITTER

While renaming oneself is an exaggerated trend today, it has been a common practice since ancient times. In the first chapter of the Book of Ruth, written centuries before Christ, we discover that Naomi, Ruth's mother-in-law, had not only lost her husband but also both of her sons and was experiencing her own identity crisis. All she had left were the clothes on her back and the unconditional love and loyalty of her daughter-in-law. During their journey back to Naomi's hometown of Bethlehem, an interesting exchange took place, revealing her state of mind.

> When they arrived in Bethlehem, the whole town was stirred because of them, and the women exclaimed, "Can this be Naomi?"
>
> "Don't call me Naomi," she told them. "Call me Mara, because the Almighty has made my life very bitter. I went away full, but the Lord has brought me back empty. Why call me Naomi?"
>
> Ruth 1: 19-21

Naomi changed her name based on her pain. The name *Mara* means *bitterness* while her God-given name *Naomi* means *my delight*. How many times have we done this? During challenging and disappointing times, when circumstances don't align with our desires, we tend to rename ourselves to express our pain and frustration: overlooked, forgotten, poor, useless.

> "Only the Creator can rightly define His creation."

Or perhaps we rename ourselves based on our feelings? As a result, we might change our name to match how we feel inside so that our external identity aligns with our inner emotions. Who hasn't struggled with believing names like, *I am unloved; I am rejected; I am a victim*? Each of these views is more than a mere statement we would think or say to ourselves; it is an assignment of a name. Unloved. Rejected. Victim. It's crucial to recognize these "I am" statements as the lies they are and replace them with God's "I am" statements.

YOU ARE QUALIFIED IN JESUS

Nothing can disqualify you from being who the Lord says you are unless you allow it—not your family, heritage, education, gender, age, traditions of man—nothing disqualifies in and of itself. The Lord never defines us by our outward circumstances and neither should we. He looks at who He says we are, and this is how He defines and relates to us. A good friend of ours, Jim Baker, says it perfectly: "Never look at yourself apart from Christ because God never does." To run the race that God has set before us, we must cast off anything that hinders us, including external beliefs, false expectations, opinions of others, and even our own histories in order to run the race He has set before us. Believe His voice above all others. Every person will stand before the Lord one day and give an account of the race they have run. May none of us hear Him say, "You were running a good race. Who cut in on you to keep you from obeying the truth?"[4]

The truth is, we weren't designed to live bound by internal or external labels, restrictions, or limitations. Rather, we should aim to live in alignment with the truth of our eternal identity, the heavenly reality unveiling our truest self. Only He can reveal that to us.

While breaking free from boxes is vitally important, it will not benefit us if we don't embrace the eternal truth of who God created us to be. In the upcoming chapters, we will dive into the significance of our heavenly identity and explore how God reveals our unique identity through our names.

CHAPTER REFLECTIONS

What do you believe is the biggest external box you face right now and why?

_____
_____
_____
_____

Have you ever placed an external box on someone else through teasing, nicknames, or lesser opinions of who they are? If so, what were these labels, and what should you do about it?

_____
_____
_____
_____

One of the challenges in our culture today is the external boxes people place on their view of God. What can you say or do to help break these boxes and release the truth of who God is in the world around you?

_____
_____
_____
_____

CHAPTER END NOTES

---

1. 1 Corinthians 3:19.

2. Judges 6:12.

3. 2 Corinthians 5:16.

4. Galatians 5:7.

Chapter 4

Scripture Reveals Your Last Name

Now that you have broken off the lies and misdirection on your path, it's time to explore the initial phases of your identity treasure map. The first step in discovering the power of your heavenly identity through your name is to explore the distinctive qualities of the Kingdom family you now belong to. In the natural realm, family names help to define generational skills, qualities, and values of a lineage. Just as the Bible reveals the physical genealogy of Jesus (you know, those long lists of His ancestors' names), scripture also provides a sort of spiritual genealogy or family association for all believers.

There are many names of qualities that make up our spiritual family heritage. When scripture describes what a son or daughter in the kingdom of God looks like, it's essentially telling you something about your spiritual last name. The Kingdom family name tells every son and daughter of God who they are, what their family traits are, and what the values of their heavenly home are.

YOUR FAMILY NAMES

In the natural world, our last names or surnames link us with our family line. Your last name connects you to your parents, siblings, cousins, grandparents and even that weird aunt or uncle you see only once a year. The common thread of connection is your shared story, DNA, and your last name. But there can also be similarities in appearance, behaviors, gifts, and even tendencies towards certain vocations within a family line.

Recently, there was a story of two brothers who were separated during World War II. One was sent to the countryside of Europe, and the other came to America to escape the Nazi invasion. The brothers lost touch and didn't reconnect until they were in their sixties. Through DNA and ancestry research, the American brother located the other and asked him to visit.

When the day of the meeting arrived, the American and his wife stood anxiously at the airport, watching the people arrive at the baggage claim. Suddenly, the husband exclaimed, "That's my brother!" The wife asked, "How do you know? He looks nothing like you."

"I know it is him," the brother explained. "He walks like my father."

In the spiritual world, the "last names" given to believers in scripture as children of God are so we can walk like our Father. These names and spiritual titles connect us not only to our heavenly Father but also to one another as family. The Book of Ephesians confirms that we have received our family name from our heavenly Father.

> For this reason, I kneel before the Father, from whom every family in heaven and on earth derives its name. (Ephesians 3:14-15)

Regardless of whether you come from a loving and godly natural family or prefer to forget your earthly family history, Jesus has wiped the slate clean for us all. You have a new family now and as a born-again believer come under the honor and influence of a new family name. Every single person on this planet who longs to discover where they belong can find the answer to this question in God's family. For those who believe, God has given us His family name(s) that carries and conveys all the blessings, authority, and identity attached to sons and daughters of God.

Let's explore just a few of the names that describe the family of God in which you are part:

Child of God: This is the starting place for every believer. We are no longer orphans but sons and daughters of the living God.[1] Child of God is no small title. The born-again experience has made us new creations[2] with the very nature[3] and righteousness of God Himself.[4]

Co-heirs with Christ: As sons and daughters, we now share in the inheritance of Jesus. This means that everything that belongs to Jesus also belongs to you.[5]

Ambassadors for Christ: You are an accredited authority to carry out the business of Heaven on the earth.[6] You are a governmental authority of the ministry of Jesus Christ.

Citizens of Heaven: Having traveled to six continents and dozens of countries, we have loved every nation we've been to. We are impressed by the people, the culture, the architecture, the food–all that makes it unique. But as much as we love these nations, we would never be allowed to vote in an election there since we have no authority or legal right to. We can only vote in the United States where we are citizens. We may not have voting rights in the kingdom of Heaven (as it is not a democracy), but as its citizens, we do have authority to release Heaven's atmosphere, will, and ways into the world around us.[7]

Friends of Christ: We are no longer slaves who do not know what our Master is up to. As friends, we have access to His thoughts, His will, and His heart.[8]

A New Creation: You are a new type of created being in Christ Jesus with dual citizenship in Heaven and on earth.[9]

Saints: Have you heard the statement that we are all just sinners saved by grace? To the contrary, believers once were sinners, but are no longer. Now we are called to be saints.[10] Does that mean we never sin or miss the mark? Of course not, but *sinner* is no longer our identity. Believers do not live to the fullest of their heavenly identity when they call themselves something the Father does not.

Light of the World: Because of the radiance of the Son of God living within us, when we love like Jesus does, we shine like Him too. This dark and desperate world is longing for you to be the light of the world He says you are.[11]

As believers, we often skim over the identities found in scripture, not realizing that each name is an invitation to discover who we are and who our family is. Every name is a powerful declaration of our heavenly identity and purpose on earth. To walk in the fullness promised to us in Christ Jesus, we must learn to walk out our family names found in scripture.

ON EARTH AS IN HEAVEN

We begin to truly be the Body of Christ on earth by shifting our mindset to embrace who the Father says we are as the family of God and then allowing that renewed mind to transform our behavior. It's not enough to have head knowledge of our Kingdom surnames; we must understand that we have been grafted into this vine, that we are now part of the family line, and that we carry the nature and characteristics of the family. You were created to walk like your heavenly Father. The great prayer of Jesus is, "Let Your will be done on earth as it is in Heaven."[12] If you want earth to look more like Heaven, one of the most practical ways to do that is to start living from your heavenly family name.

> "If you want earth to look more like Heaven, start living from your heavenly family name."

These last names belong to you as a believer. Jesus already qualified you through adoption. You cannot disqualify yourself. You aren't disowned by the family when you make bad choices. If our children make outrageously poor decisions, there would be consequences to their actions, but their last name would not change. It's the same with us as God's children. You may feel at times that you don't deserve to bear the name, but the truth is it's when we come to agreement with our heavenly surnames that we begin to live from them and not for them.

ASSERTING YOUR FAMILY NAME *(Bethany)*

Many years ago, I was in Australia participating at a conference hosted by a powerful prophet, worship leader, and good friend, Roma Waterman. As the conference came to a close, there was a large group of volunteer workers in the speakers' private room who began to clean up. I noticed our host's pre-teen daughter stood up and began cleaning and putting things away. One of the volunteers made a comment to her along the lines of, "Hey sweetie, you don't need to clean up. We've got helpers for that!" The young girl turned to the leader and replied, "I'm a Waterman, this is what we do."'

No one asked her to help nor did her parents make a demand on her; she chose to help because that's what her family does. The Watermans love others by serving and helping whoever and whenever they can. This young daughter had a strong understanding of who her family had chosen to be, and she was living from the power and authority of that identity.

When you show up knowing what it means to be God's son or daughter, you will manifest your Kingdom family's identity and purpose. Are you dealing with some tough and dark circumstances? Then say your name: "I am the light of the world. I shine in the darkness. This is what we do as the family of God." You are there because you shine, and your very presence in the room causes darkness to flee.

Or perhaps you need a miracle or some major provision for a God-sized vision. Then say your name: "I'm a co-heir with Christ. I have access to everything I need for what He has called me to do. I don't shrink back. This is what we do." When you begin to believe that everything that belongs to Jesus also belongs to you, you will appropriate that identity by speaking forth with confidence what He says about your situation.

In pursuing this discovery of the names God calls us, we must understand that they hold more value than just being endearing labels. Every name is a precious gem that contributes to the treasure that is your unique and royal identity. Each name holds a key that propels you towards fulfilling your

God-given purpose and destiny. And every name marks the boundary lines of what you are responsible for and what you have authority to do. For these reasons, we must both passionately pursue who He says we are and reject every inferior name. Our destinies depend on it.

> "Each name holds a key that propels you toward fulfilling your God-given purpose and destiny."

It's time to believe what you've already received through Christ and start owning your last name. Earth is groaning for the sons and daughters of God to know who they are.[13] Dive into the Word of God and discover all the family names you already have and enjoy the discovery of your truest self in the process. I am a child of God; this is what we do.

CHAPTER REFLECTIONS

Look at the short list of family names in this chapter. Which of these family-of-God identities speaks most to your situation right now and what lie is it displacing for you? What other family-of-God last name identities found in scripture are being highlighted to you about yourself right now?

_____

_____

_____

_____

Reminding one another who we are in Christ Jesus is a powerful way to live in Christian community. Who in your circle of family and friends needs to be reminded of who God says they are? What specifically could you share with them from this chapter?

_____

_____

_____

_____

Our last names as adopted sons and daughters of God are one of the great privileges which we can thank God for. Take a moment now to write a prayer of thanksgiving to God for the names He has bestowed on you.

_____

_____

_____

_____

CHAPTER END NOTES

_____

1. Galatians 3:26.

2. 2 Corinthians 5:17.

3. 2 Peter 1:4.

4. 2 Corinthians 5:21.

5. Romans 8:17.

6. 2 Corinthians 5:20.

7. Philippians 3:20-21.

8. John 15:15.

9. 2 Corinthians 5:17.

10. 1 Corinthians 1:2.

11. Matthew 5:13-16.

12. Matthew 5:13-16.

13. Romans 8:19.

Chapter 5

Prophecy Reveals Your First Name

We are on a treasure hunt to know our heavenly identity—who Heaven says we are. As we learned in the last chapter, part of our heavenly identity can be found in the names that scripture has revealed as belonging to the family of believers. These identities along with their related authorities and responsibilities are inherently ours as members of the family of God. These titles and descriptions are collectively our Kingdom last name. Yet, this is only part of the heavenly identity package for us. The family names describe every son and daughter of God, but first names or given names speak to who you are uniquely and what you are specifically put on the earth to do.

In the same way that the written word of God reveals our spiritual last name, the spoken word of God prophetically reveals our first name. The written word displays the authority of our corporate identity — who we are as the family of God — while the prophetic word shows us individually who we are and the unique gifts we carry to serve the world. Let's explore this further, but before we do, we'll clarifying some misconceptions about the biblical gift of prophecy.

PROPHECY DEFINED

Prophecy, simply defined, is accessing the thoughts, the voice, and the heart of God through the power of the Holy Spirit. Prophecy is what God is currently saying about you. The truest thing about you in the universe is who God says you are. The spiritual gift of prophecy is available to every son and daughter of God as promised through the predictions of the prophet Joel:

> And afterward, I will pour out my Spirit on all people. Your sons and daughters will prophesy....
>
> Joel 2:28

The Book of Acts in the New Testament reveals that this prophecy was fulfilled on the Day of Pentecost during the first century AD when Peter stood and said,

> But this is what was uttered through the prophet Joel: "And in the last days it shall be," God declares, "that I will pour out my Spirit on all flesh, and your sons and your daughters shall prophesy...."
>
> Acts 2:16-17 ESV

Several important things are clear in these passages. First, this promise has been fulfilled and the gift of prophecy is currently available. Secondly, this promise is for all believers. The only other requirement is flesh. It is God's purpose, will, and work that has caused this gracious outpouring upon all people. In the previous chapter, we focused on the benefits of being part of God's family. As children of God, we have the grace and privilege of accessing His thoughts, His voice, and His heart as promised in the scripture "your sons and daughters shall prophesy..."

ACCESS TO GOD'S VOICE *(Dano)*

Jesus said plainly, "My sheep know my voice."[1] That's a statement of fact. There was a time in my life where this verse caused insecurity. I reasoned, "I'm not hearing or discerning His voice so I must not be His sheep." This lie plagued my sense of security and belonging in the family of God. Then, the Holy Spirit taught me to reverse the phrase into a declaration, "Because I am His sheep, I do hear His voice!" I start with confidence, not in myself, but in the work of Christ and what He has said. If you question whether you truly hear God's voice, I recommend you do the same thing. Flip the script and trust in what God has done in saving you.

Jesus is the Good Shepherd who has made us His sheep, granting us the ability to access and follow His voice. The problem is never getting God to speak because God is always speaking. The challenge is merely in recognizing all the ways that God is already speaking and learning to respond to His voice.

Not only do you have access to the voice of God; you also have the mind of Christ.[2] Paul's letter to the Corinthian church clearly states that the Holy Spirit is revealing the thoughts of God to us because we have been given the mind of Christ. We share these things so that you can confidently partner in discovering your heavenly identity and destiny through the spiritual gift of prophecy. Every son and daughter can clearly and confidently know the voice, the thoughts, and the heart of God through the redeeming work of Jesus Christ and the outpouring of the Holy Spirit on all people.

DISCERNING GOD'S VOICE

Our access to the voice of God does not imply that His will be the only voice that speaks to you. On the other hand, God does speak to you; and the devil will attempt to cast doubt on what you have heard from God. In the Garden of Eden, the original temptation was that of uncertainty. The devil asked Eve, "Did God really say?" The enemy of your soul wants you to doubt your ability to hear God and your confidence to trust what He has said.

The spiritual battle arises because Satan understands that God's voice is a powerful creative force in the universe. In the beginning, God's words brought worlds into being, and His voice continues to shape and define our world today. What God speaks shifts reality. When we align ourselves with God's words, our reality undergoes a transformation.

> "God's words brought worlds into being, and His voice continues to shape and define our world today."

SORTING OUT THE VOICES

So how do you sort out God's voice from your own, the voice of others, or the deceptions and temptations of the devil? First Thessalonians 5:20-21 encourages believers to test prophetic words. We want to share four simple criteria for judging what you feel you are hearing from God.

First, a word of prophecy will never contradict the written word of scripture. Though there may not always be a specific scriptural reference for every prophecy, both the scripture and prophecy come from the same divine source. Moreover, since the Spirit and the Truth are one, they will never contradict each other. If you ever receive a prophecy that goes against what is written in the Bible, you can be certain that it did not come from the Lord.

Second, no word of prophecy will contradict the character and nature of God. In other words, it should sound like something a loving Father would say to His children. I Corinthians 13, the famous love chapter, teaches us that all spiritual gifts must operate within the boundaries of God's love, or they are meaningless. Love is defined as patient, kind, and selfless, among other things.

Many prophecies in the Old Testament were intertwined with warnings and judgments of a covenant intended to demonstrate the outcome of a life lived apart from God. However, we are now in a New Covenant reality, and the purpose of prophecy is to encourage, strengthen, and comfort the believer[3] in the realities of a life sanctified and united with Christ. Jesus fulfilled the Old Covenant so He could establish the new, and this includes the purpose and protocols of prophecy.

A third criteria for knowing you are hearing the voice of God through prophecy is that it will bear witness with you. Scripture tells us that the same Spirit that raised Christ from the dead lives in us.[4] His Spirit testifies to our spirit that we are the children of God.[5] In the Book of Acts, the New Testament believers would make decisions based upon the witness of the Spirit within them. They said, "It seemed good to us and to the Holy Spirit…"[6] The inner witness of the Holy Spirit can come as a sense that the prophetic word given to you is true and that it applies to you.

Additionally, prophecy should manifest the fruit of the Spirit within you with a witness of love, joy, peace, patience, kindness, goodness, gentleness, faithfulness, and self-control. These inner witnesses serve as confirmation that we are indeed receiving a message from God.[7]

Lastly, judging prophecy is not just a matter of your own internal witness; major life decisions should always be made with the input and counsel of others. The early church pattern was "Let two or three prophets prophesy, and let the rest weight carefully what was said."[8] We should not follow a prophecy that pulls us away from the wise counsel of loved ones and leaders. There are times when we must stand alone in believing, but it is the exception not the norm for clearly discerning the voice of God. Whenever there is a question about the accuracy or implementation of a prophetic word, we should include the counsel of other godly people in our decisions.[9]

With this generous gift of God and healthy protocols in place, we can now move forward in discovering the various ways that God speaks individually to each person's identity and destiny. What God calls you uniquely through a word of prophecy is not necessarily what He would say to every other member of the family. It is a specific and unique call for you as an individual member of God's family. In this way, it is like a spiritual first name because it is something that gives you distinction and purpose within the greater family of sons and daughters. Let's look at some personal examples.

WORSHIP LEADING PROPHET *(Bethany)*

For over twenty years, I served as a worship pastor and director in many churches of various sizes and locations. I loved every minute of it even with its occupational challenges. About a decade ago, a prophet came to my little mountain church and prophesied a new heavenly name over me that radically shifted my identity. He said, "Bethany, you're not a worship leader who prophesies; you're a prophet who leads worship."

The force of those words coming from the heart of the Father hit my spirit like a sledgehammer. I could feel the weight of truth behind that statement, and it was more than semantics. The Lord was revealing to me my heavenly identity, and I had a choice to step into the truth of my new name of prophet.

You see, as a worship leader who prophesied, I was continually looking for what the Lord would want to speak through the songs, through the atmosphere, or through my prophetic perceptions. Affecting the spiritual atmosphere as a worship leader always felt more "outside-in," as if the prophetic was outside of me and I was searching for it. But now seeing myself as a prophet who leads worship, I realize that I am the very conduit that God is speaking through. Previously, as a worship leader who prophesied I was looking for the breakthrough; but now, as a prophet who leads worship, I am the breakthrough in Him!

Therefore, it does not matter which song I lead because at the very strum of my guitar, prophetic grace is released. At the first note, God will be singing through me. That's not a statement of arrogance but one of confidence that comes from embracing a new identity from my heavenly Father.

This is the power of the prophetic! In that moment ten plus years ago, God pulled back the curtain of how Heaven saw me. Through the encouraging gift of prophecy, He revealed a prophetic first name that expanded my understanding of who He has created me to be.

ME, A PROPHET? *(Dano)*

Years ago, a friend invited me to help him found Bethel School of the Prophets. I told him, "I'm happy to help you teach, but I don't think I'm a prophet."

He replied, "Don't you go to other nations and call out worship leaders who then become the primary voice in their nation?"

"Yes," I answered.

"Well, that's a prophet," he said, "Just shut up and do it!"

Nevertheless, for the first few years of teaching in the school, I didn't believe I was a prophet. I knew my friend loved me, and I reasoned that he, knowing I was a good teacher, just wanted us to build something together.

Three years into the School of the Prophets, we invited a third speaker to join us. I knew the guest speaker from previous interactions, but we hadn't seen each other in several years, so he had no personal knowledge of what I had recently been up to. In the first few minutes of the introduction to his teaching, the prophet said, "Dano, stand to your feet." I stood up in obedience. "The Lord says, 'You are a prophet after the order of Asaph, restoring the Levitical priesthood and rebuilding David's Tabernacle.'" He went on to describe everything I was building through worship in the nations at that time. In that moment, I saw the connection with my call as a prophet. I accepted the name that God was wanting to call me by.

I don't know why I didn't believe my prophet friend through conversation; but I did believe the guest prophet through the declared prophetic word. My point is this: I didn't see myself the way that God saw me. I knew what I was building and that it was a good Kingdom thing, but I didn't know I was building it as a prophet. Since that realization, I have not only been able to help worshipers and musicians, but I have literally equipped tens of thousands of people on six continents how to recognize and respond to the voice of God in prophecy. The prophetic word defined something I was already living the beginnings of, but the prophetic name gave it new clarity and authority.

> "There are things about you in which you will never live to their full potential until God defines them for you."

Prophetic or heavenly identity, however, is not just for prophets or people in vocational ministry. God wants to speak prophetically to every person in each sector of humanity. The power of prophetic identity is in the fact that God sees who you really are and desires to call it out. There are things about you in which you will never live to their full potential until God defines them for you. God not only wants us all to live in the dignity and virtues that every son and daughter can enjoy, but He also desires to reveal the unique world-changer qualities He crafted into you. The Book of Ephesians says, "For we are his workmanship, having been created in Christ Jesus for good works that God prepared beforehand so that we may do them."[10]

You see, your heavenly identity is seen in the unique ways God wants to express His own character and nature through you. We each carry a special fragrance of Christ to the world.[11] These distinct qualities that God has put into each of us have the power to change the world. Prophecy is a primary way that these qualities are revealed and activated.

In the next three chapters, we will explore three ways to understand the prophetic significance of your natural given name to reveal additional pieces to the treasure map of your heavenly identity.

CHAPTER REFLECTIONS

How confident are you in your ability to hear God's voice regarding the promises He has made to those who are born again?

_____

_____

_____

_____

Think about the people around you who need an upgraded sense of their heavenly identity. Write out the names of three to five friends and family members who you would like to target with prophetic blessings and insights through the skills you are learning.

_____

_____

_____

_____

God is constantly revealing secrets of His own identity. There are hundreds of descriptions of God in the Bible and each one is an invitation to an encounter. Ask God who He wants to be for you right now and write down the answer below along with any revelations of why and how He will be that for you.

CHAPTER END NOTES

1. John 10:4, 27.

2. 1 Corinthians 2:16.

3. 1 Corinthians 14:3.

4. Romans 8:11.

5. Romans 8:16.

6. Acts 15:28.

7. James 3:17.

8. 1 Corinthians 14:29.

9. See also Proverbs 1:5, 11:14, 12:15, 15:22, 20:18, 24:6.

10. Ephesians 2:10.

11. 2 Corinthians 2:14-15.

Chapter 6

The Meaning of Your Name

Your heavenly identity is not only found in what God calls you but also in how your heavenly Father views the name you were given at birth. The treasure of who God made you to be is woven into the meaning of your name. You are not an accident. No human being is just another name or number on the earth. Each person is crafted by the Lord with unique qualities and purpose. To gain a deeper understanding of your original design, the next step is to explore the prophetic meaning of your earthly name. By delving into God's intention behind the meaning of your name, you can uncover powerful insights into your unique purpose and potential. Discovering identity and purpose through name meaning is not a fabricated idea from man's imagination, but rather an age-old revelation of how God connects with us through our names.

In chapter one, we discussed how God reveals His nature through the meaning of His own names. For example, Jehovah Jireh means that God can see in advance and have provision waiting for us while Jehovah Rapha means that it is in God's nature to heal and restore. Each of God's names is a revelation of both who He is and what He is capable of. We also looked at examples from the lives of Eve, Moses, Esther, David, and Barnabas to show how the meanings of their names related to their nature, identity, and destiny.

Does this mean that God caused us to be named a certain way or that He knew our names before we were born? To answer this question, we must first understand that God does not live within the same constructs and boundaries of time as we do. The One who was, who is, and who is to come, knew and called you before time began. He can see the past, the present, and a potential future simultaneously. He may not have chosen or influenced what you would be named, but He chose *you*, and He has a powerful way of relating to your name. Paul the apostle says it this way, "He chose us in Him before the creation of the world...."[1] You were chosen even before a single particle of matter existed. This is evident in God's words to the ancient prophet Jeremiah.

> Before I formed you in the womb I knew you, before you were born, I set you apart; I appointed you as a prophet to the nations.
>
> Jeremiah 1:5

In Hebrew, Jeremiah's name literally means "*whom Jehovah has appointed.*"[2] Within the call of God on Jeremiah's life the Lord used the exact meaning of Jeremiah's name to reaffirm both his identity as a prophet and his call to the nations.

God did not just foreknow Jeremiah as some vague and impersonal reference to his physical existence. The Almighty God of Heaven was intimately acquainted with Jeremiah's identity and destiny before his birth because the Creator intentionally crafted every facet of Jeremiah's gifts, his call, and yes, even what would be associated with his name. Therefore, within Jeremiah's name lay the seeds of his identity and destiny waiting to be discovered and walked out on earth. It is the same with us.

GOD'S KNOWING IN ADVANCE

King Josiah is another example of God's amazing foreknowledge. At least three hundred years before the birth of Josiah, a prophet from Judah said, "A son named Josiah will be born to the house of David."[3] He prophesied before Jeroboam who was one of Judah's most wicked kings that this coming king would eliminate the false priests and altar of idolatry. Josiah's name means *whom Jehovah heals*.[4] God foreknew that a king would come whom He could support and who would heal the nation, and God knew his name would be Josiah.

God's foreknowledge does not mean that we are all merely living out a pre-written script; we each have choice and responsibility to align with our God-given potential and purpose. Some will choose to follow this treasure map, and others will wander from their design.

> "We each have choice and responsibility to align with our God-given potential and purpose."

God's intentionality with names and name meanings is certainly displayed in the life of Jesus. When Joseph was contemplating quietly breaking off his relationship with Mary, an angel of the Lord appeared to him in a dream saying,

> Joseph, son of David, do not be afraid to take to you Mary your wife, for that which is conceived in her is of the Holy Spirit. And she will bring forth a Son, and you shall call His name Jesus, for He will save His people from their sins.
>
> Matthew 1:20-21

God ordained that the child would be named *Jesus* which means *Jehovah is salvation* because He would save people from sin. As Jesus' heavenly Father, He had the right to name His Son as fathers often did in that culture, and He did so very intentionally, knowing the power that a name carries.

We are not necessarily saying that God has pre-ordained the exact name of every child ever born, but we are saying that He knows each name and has considered it in each one's unique design. Because God knew and chose us before the foundations of the world, our names are more than coincidence. Our names are not just a result of our parents being influenced by baby name trends of our birth year. The impact of your name is not limited to your parents' motivation in choosing it. Rather, God has a heavenly thought and plan associated with each name. Every name, regardless of its origin, carries a greater prophetic significance in how it relates to our identity than perhaps we have imagined.

GOD SPEAKS THROUGH NAME MEANINGS

Abraham is known throughout history as a father of the faith. That title is intricately linked to the meaning of his own name. God appeared to Abram and announced that his future would soon take a dramatic turn. This shift in destiny is rooted in the meaning of his name. The name *Abram* meant *exalted father* in Hebrew.[5] However, God had an even grander plan for him.

> Abram fell facedown, and God said to him, "As for me, this is the covenant with you: You will be the father of many nations. No longer will you be called Abram; your name will be Abraham, for I have made you a father of many nations."
>
> Genesis 17: 3-5

God took the name and its meaning and upgraded it to another level, giving him the name *Abraham* meaning *exalted father of a multitude*.[6] Despite being an exalted father in some sense, Abram had yet to fulfill God's prophetic promise of becoming a father of many nations. While he was respected as Ishmael's father and as a father figure by his servants, his destiny as the father of nations rested on the future birth of Isaac. God not only unveiled the treasure of Abram's identity through his name, but He also upgraded the name and its meaning to announce an even bigger and brighter future.

Abram wasn't the only one who received a prophetic name upgrade. His wife, Sarai, also received a new name as this future promise also belonged to her.

> God also said to Abraham, "As for Sarai your wife, you are no longer to call her Sarai; her name will be Sarah...she will be the mother of nations...."
>
> Genesis 17:15-16

Sarai means *princess*, but as she came into an even greater leadership role in history, she was promoted to Sarah meaning *noble woman*. As God unlocked and upgraded the meaning in Abraham's and Sarah's names, it unleashed a perspective shift of their heavenly identity so they could embrace the greater destiny God had prepared for them.

This story powerfully demonstrates how God uses the meaning of a name to convey a prophetic message about a person's identity and destiny. Just as Abraham and Sarah experienced, God has greater plans and purposes for us that are waiting to be revealed through prophetic revelation found in our names.

JESUS USES NAME MEANINGS

Jesus also used name meanings to lay out maps of identity and destiny in the New Testament. In one instance, He asked His disciples who they believed Him to be. When Simon Peter answered correctly saying, "You are the Messiah, the Son of the living God," Jesus turned to him and prophesied by pulling out the meaning of the name Peter.

> And I tell you that you are Peter, and on this rock I will build my church, and the gates of Hades will not overcome it. I will give you the keys of the kingdom of heaven; whatever you bind on earth will be bound in heaven, and whatever you loose on earth will be loosed in heaven.
> Matthew 16: 17-19

Peter means *a rock or a stone.*[7] Jesus prophesied that on this rock (the revelation of Jesus as Messiah and Son of the living God), Jesus would build His church. The rock-solid revelation of the identity of Jesus came from the mouth of one whose name was *rock*.

ISRAEL BLESSES THROUGH NAME MEANINGS

The twelve tribes of Israel also have a link to prophetic meanings within their names. In the Book of Genesis, Jacob spoke prophetic blessings over many of his sons based on the meanings of their names. He told them, "Gather around so I can tell you what will happen to you in days to come." To *Judah* whose name means *praise*, he said, "Your brothers will praise you." To *Dan* whose name means *judge*, Jacob said, "Dan will provide justice for his people." The elder of Israel continued his prophetic blessings until he had addressed each of his sons according to their names.[8] These blessings affected the identity and destiny of the tribes of Israel for hundreds of years following. The Bible holds a treasure of names with their prophetic meanings if we would but dig through the nuances of the ancient Hebrew and Greek languages.

ETHAN, STRONG AND STEADFAST *(Bethany)*

This ancient principle of the power of name meanings still affects the maps of our identities and destinies today. My son was named very intentionally when he was born. His name *Ethan* means *strong and steadfast*. Ethan was also the name of one of the chief musicians in the Book of Psalms. As my son grew up, I observed a firmness and stability of character in him. He is immovable when it comes to his values or principles. He displays an unwavering and persistent nature in all his endeavors and never bows to peer pressure.

A few years ago, when he was a high school senior, we were

praying about his next steps after graduation. It was during this time of prayer that Ethan came home from school one day after attending a college fair where he had spoken with a navy recruiter. Ethan then announced that he intended to join the U.S. Navy after he graduated. This news came as a shock to me as I had not considered the military as a potential career path for him. While I am deeply grateful for the sacrifice and service of those who serve in the military, as a mother, my primary concern was for my son's safety, and joining the military did not seem like a secure option to me.

As I dialogued with the Lord about my son's decision to join the U.S. Navy, I internally heard the Lord ask me, "Do you remember what you used to declare over him when he was a little boy?" Instantly, I saw a picture of him wrestling a little too aggressively with his younger sisters. Whenever that happened, I would pull him aside and reaffirm his name's meaning to him by saying, "Hey, buddy. God did not make you strong to be a bully. He made you strong to be a defender of the defenseless."

The Lord used this memory to reveal to me the prophetic identity attached to my son's name and affirm that his decision to join the military was aligned with his destiny. What better way for my son to be a defender of the defenseless than by serving in the military for the protection and defense of our country? This revelation brought so much peace as God confirmed to me that my son was on the right path, and He did it through the power of the prophetic meaning of his name.

REDEEMING JUSTICE *(Bethany)*

Recently, I was drawn to a policeman who had parked his car at a local school, so I pulled over to ask him some questions. While we were talking, I noticed that the name on his uniform read Officer J. Villain.[9] Noting his last name, I commented on the irony of his surname being Villain while his job involves catching criminals. He chuckled and mentioned that he had frequently been teased about it.

A few minutes later, he handed me his business card, and I noticed that his full name was Justin Villain. I asked the officer if he knew the meaning of his first name, to which he replied that he did not. "*Justin* means *just and fair*," I told him. "You've only seen half of the picture; your first and last names put together literally mean *justice to villains*!" This police officer was manifesting the prophetic power of his name.

He was incredibly excited about this revelation, and you could see in his countenance how redeeming this encounter was for him. The teasing he'd endured over his last name was now inconsequential in light of a more complete understanding. His first name paired with his last name prophetically connected the dots to a more complete picture of his full identity, and he would no longer view his name negatively. That is the prophetic power of a name's meaning.

CHRISTOPHER CHRISTMAS

There is a man in the Austin, Texas, area who looks just like a Norman Rockwell depiction of Santa Claus. He's got a round happy face with white hair, a full beard, rectangular spectacles, the proper body shape, and often wears suspenders. He exudes a warmth and kindness that draws the attention and trust of young and old alike. When we first met him, we were shocked to discover that his given name was Christopher Carol Christmas. Incredulously, he didn't change his name to match his persona. This name was assigned by his parents at birth which can be verified on his birth certificate. Today, Christopher serves as a professional Santa releasing the love of Jesus as the Christ-bearer he is. He is intentionally walking in the power of his name.

How can you begin to unlock the treasure of identity and destiny in your name's meaning? Start by looking up the meaning of your first, last, and even middle names on the internet or in a name encyclopedia. There are often many root words and various meanings for each name, but they are usually similar enough to give a broad idea to start with. Pay attention also to the name's meaning according to your original heritage or ethnicity. Then—and here is the most important key—ask the Holy Spirit what He is unveiling about your identity and destiny through the meaning of your name.

UNLOCKING THE TREASURE *(Dano)*

My last name, *McCollam*, comes from an English root meaning *column* or *strong like a pillar*. That speaks to the strength and resolve of the McCollam family line. Can you imagine the strength and support one might feel if they understood and leaned into that meaning in their family name? But the name is also Irish, and the Gaelic meaning of *McCollam* is *son of Columba*. Saint Columba is credited with bringing the Gospel to Ireland, and the name literally means *dove*. Therefore, my last name also means *son of the dove*. Biblically, a dove often represents the Holy Spirit, and anyone who knows me can see the connection between my love for the Gospel, my missionary spirit, and my friendship with the Holy Spirit.

I was living intuitively from the power of my name's meaning long before I fully understood it. However, gaining prophetic understanding unlocked another measure of confidence and authority.

WHAT DOES GOD SAY?

In conclusion, we can see in the Bible that God prophesied over Abraham and Sarah according to the meanings of their names. The Angel of the Lord spoke to both Mary and Joseph about the identity and destiny of Jesus based upon the meaning of His name. Jesus prophesied an earth-shaking destiny over Simon Peter based upon the meaning of his name. Repeated patterns and typologies in scripture reveal wisdom keys of how name meanings can unlock heavenly blessings. As we understand the pattern of prophesying through a name's meaning, we find the power to unlock the heavenly secrets of our own identities and destinies.

> "Heavenly identity comes from a prophetic understanding of what God is speaking through your name."

Take note, however, that human assumptions derived from name meaning do not have the power to define us. Heavenly identity comes from a prophetic understanding of what God is speaking through your name. Don't just look up your name's meaning and start drawing conclusions. The power is in what the Holy Spirit is saying. Look up the meaning of your name, then ask the Holy Spirit how this meaning relates to who you are and what God has called you to be. Take time to watch and listen for all the instructions God wants to reveal in your treasure map. Allow other believers to share what they are receiving from the Lord prophetically about your name and add those pieces to your treasure map. Remember that the purpose of prophecy in the New Testament is to encourage, strengthen, and comfort, so any prophetic meaning attached to a name must be redemptive and follow love's protocol.

Name meaning is a powerful tool for understanding who God created you to be and what He has for you to do. But it is also an amazing tool for serving and adding value to people and places around you. Everyone is searching for meaning and purpose. Prophesying the redemptive meaning of another person's name can be a game-changer for shaping who God says they are and what purposes He has uniquely suited them for.

Prophesying from name meanings is a powerful life skill that is supported by its vast use in the Bible. Name meaning is clearly one of the ways that God speaks to identity and purpose. Let's use this knowledge to increase our conversations with the Holy Spirit and add strength, encouragement, and comfort to one another through prophetic blessings based on the meaning of a name.

CHAPTER REFLECTIONS

Look up the meaning of your name if you don't already know it. Ask Holy Spirit how it speaks to your heavenly identity and destiny. Take some time to look and listen for His voice, then write your impression in the space below.

_____

_____

_____

_____

Recall the names of the people you wrote down in the last chapter reflection and look up the meanings of their names. Now ask Holy Spirit to show you how their name meanings relate to the treasure of their heavenly identity, and write the information below.

_____

_____

_____

_____

Take the name of God that He shared with you in the reflection section of the last chapter which represents who He wants to be for you right now. Look up the meanings of that name and read the passages where it appears in scripture. Through this research, ask Holy Spirit to expand your understanding of who God wants to be for you, and yield yourself to Him through what is revealed. Write your upgraded impressions below.

CHAPTER END NOTES

1. Ephesians 1:4.

2. H3414 - yirmᵊyâ - Strong's Hebrew Lexicon (niv). Retrieved from https://www.blueletterbible.org/lexicon/h3414/niv/wlc/0-1/.

3. 1 Kings 13:1.

4. H2977 - yō'šîyâ - Strong's Hebrew Lexicon (niv). Retrieved from https://www.blueletterbible.org/lexicon/h2977/niv/wlc/0-1/.

5. H87 - 'aḇrām - Strong's Hebrew Lexicon (niv). Retrieved from https://www.blueletterbible.org/lexicon/h87/niv/wlc/0-1/.

6. H85 - 'aḇrāhām - Strong's Hebrew Lexicon (niv). Retrieved from https://www.blueletterbible.org/lexicon/h85/niv/wlc/0-1/.

7. G4074 - petros - Strong's Greek Lexicon (niv). Retrieved from https://www.blueletterbible.org/lexicon/g4074/niv/mgnt/0-1/.

8. Genesis 49:1-28.

9. The officer's name has been altered to protect his identity; however, the meaning of his actual name is accurately portrayed.

Chapter 7

Name Associations

Have you ever met someone who immediately reminded you of someone else, yet no one else saw the connection? You may have asked, "Don't they look just like so and so?" but no one else agreed. What happened there? You were probably seeing or perceiving an association in the spirit realm rather than the natural realm. You assumed it was a likeness connected to a similarity in appearance, but you were perceiving something familiar in a much deeper realm. God often reveals the unknown by connecting it to the familiar.

In this chapter, we'll be discussing how you can find out more about yourself and your life's purpose through the concept of name association. When we talk about name association, we're referring to the potential spiritual connections and links that exist between people, places, and organizations who bear the same name. This is also true

> "God often reveals the unknown by connecting it to the familiar."

where a prophetic word can provide insight into the connections between two individuals or places that share a common name. This is known as an "impression of association," and it has the potential to bring blessings into your life.

ASSOCIATION AND PARABLES

We can see Heaven's love for this form of communication in the way that Jesus taught through parables. He chose to make associations between familiar things—such as a seed sown or a lost sheep—and Kingdom principles that His audience did not yet know or understand. By linking the known with the unknown, the familiar with the unfamiliar, and the earthly with the heavenly, Jesus was able to communicate profound truths to His listeners.

In this way, associations are an economy of words. When the Lord connects you with a picture of something or someone that you already know well, it unlocks a vault full of thoughts, ideas, concepts, and memories associated with it. By showing you the familiar picture, God can communicate a vast amount of information and insight in a single moment. Through associations, God can intentionally download a wealth of Kingdom ideas, using personalized language, thoughts, and memories to communicate. Parable, metaphor, and association were Jesus' most common forms of communication, so it certainly is not unreasonable to believe that God still speaks to us in these ways today.

How does this work? When your brain or spirit involuntarily connects two people, places, or things, ask the Holy Spirit what He is speaking through that association. By understanding this principle of revelation through association of a person's appearance or name, we begin to discover how God speaks to us to release blessings, encouragement, and comfort over them.

CROW AND SIMON LOOK-ALIKE *(Bethany)*

Depending on their generation, many people tell me that I remind them of either the singer-songwriter Carly Simon (1970s) or Sheryl Crow (1990s). Because this happens so frequently, it's clear that there is more than a casual connection at play. Many of the people who make this visual connection have never heard or seen me function as a musician, singer, or songwriter, which I was primarily known as for over twenty years. Prophetically, there is a musical connection between my identity and destiny and these musical influencers. It is no surprise then that I have led and trained others in worship around the world and am able to affect atmospheres and create momentum through my music.

ARE YOU IRON MAN? *(Dano)*

When I was younger, I had a tightly groomed mustache and goatee that made me look like the Marvel character Iron Man. When the movies depicting Iron Man first came to the screen, several of my friends jokingly started calling me Iron Man because they thought I looked like him. One day when I took my young daughter to the park, a little girl stopped me on the playground and asked me sincerely, "Are you Iron Man?" I couldn't resist the urge and just put my finger to my mouth and said, "Shhh. Don't tell anybody." She nodded loyally and pranced off, feeling like she had a precious secret.

Days later, the Lord gently called me out for not paying attention to the deeper meaning of the association. Iron Man is known for his ability to bring innovative ideas that make things better, and the Lord was using this association with a fictional character to call me up into this part of my identity and destiny.

ASSOCIATION AND NAMES

So far, we have been discussing visual associations. However, a person or thing may or may not physically resemble another person or thing, but an involuntary association or connection is recognized in the intuitive or imaginative realm. The same thing can happen with a person's name. When you hear or read a person's name, you may immediately have an involuntary association with someone or something else that shares that name. It could be a Bible character, a historical figure, or even a friend or family member. When this type of sudden association happens, ask the Holy Spirit what the connection is between the two people who share the name.

KIM POSSIBLE *(Bethany)*

When I first met Kim, I immediately thought, "Kim Possible." Kim Possible is an animated cartoon show in the U.S.A. about a teenage girl who is a high school student by day and a superhero by night. This involuntary name association was the Lord speaking to me about how this young woman in front of me, Kim, was like a superhero with an anointing to remove the impossibilities in her path.

After I shared that prophetic encouragement based on the name association, Kim told me that she was in the middle of dealing with breast cancer. She was only in her mid-30s, and the words I shared encouraged her greatly in her identity. It wasn't so much that the Lord was revealing Himself as her healer in that moment but that she was created to do the impossible. She is Kim Possible because that's who God says she is!

About six months later, I received a message from Kim announcing that she was completely cancer-free and healthy. The prophetic association the Lord spoke through her name greatly encouraged and strengthened her during that season as she victoriously walked through that cancer diagnosis.

RESURRECTION ANOINTING *(Bethany)*

My name, Bethany, was also the name of a town in the Bible where Mary, Martha, and Lazarus lived. By the frequency of its mention and context, we can conclude that it was one of Jesus' favorite places to rest. The town is also associated with resurrection as it was the place where Jesus called Lazarus out of the grave and the site of Jesus' ascension after His resurrection. I have received prophetic words based on this association that I carry a resurrection anointing through which I bring things back to life. And do you know what? I do! I have gone into schools, churches, and ministries that were either dead or dying, and my involvement and leadership in those areas have brought these entities back to life and restored their health.

I know that when the Lord sends me to an area that is lifeless, He has anointed me with a resurrection anointing and grace to bring life.

DANIEL ASSOCIATION *(Dano)*

Many people have told me that my name, Daniel, reminds them of Daniel from the Bible. They say that I carry similar qualities of wisdom and authority and have the potential to make an impact in the lives of leaders and influencers. It's really affirming to hear that kind of feedback.

What's even more significant is that some people prophetically associate my name with the gift of interpreting dreams and understanding mysteries—just like Daniel from the Bible. All these different aspects of Daniel's life really resonate with me and encourage me to embrace my identity in Christ as revealed through these associations.

PAY ATTENTION

Pay attention to associations because they are one of the ways that God reveals His secret information to us. Associations can be a channel for prophetic information and for adding value to the people and the places around us. However, on a cautionary note, we must understand that not all thought associations are prophetic messages from the Lord. People who are hurting or untrained can make untrue associations through lenses of pain, paranoia, or rejection. Yet, when we

> "Pay attention to associations because they are one of the ways that God reveals His secret information to us."

look through the lens of God's love with the desire to encourage, comfort, and strengthen others, we often experience involuntary associations that can give us revelation into what God is saying through someone's name.

TRAIN YOURSELF

When the association that comes to mind has no obvious link to the person, seek the Lord for clarity. For instance, meeting someone named Michael might trigger thoughts of the renowned pro-basketball player Michael Jordan even if they bear no physical or athletic resemblance. Such an encounter could be an invitation from the Lord to dialog with Him about what this association might mean. The association is not always obvious regarding names or appearance.

Usually, an association or comparison, like a parable, has a single main point. So, you won't make a list of similarities, but instead, you'll be looking for the primary message that God is speaking. For instance, if your first name is Lincoln and you are drawn to the name Abraham Lincoln, the sixteenth president of the United States, there could be several potential associations. Even if you have no interest in politics, you might possess the grace to fight for unity and freedom. The president and lawyer also had a reputation as "Honest Abe," so perhaps the Lord is speaking to your trustworthiness. Lincoln was also renowned for recovering from multiple failed attempts in politics and business, but He overcame them with perseverance and resilience. He was largely self-educated but considered brilliant. You can see that there are a variety of potential associations, so it is our responsibility to ask the Holy Spirit what He is highlighting and not make human assumptions about those connections.

Think of these associative impressions as an invitation to a greater conversation with the Holy Spirit. This is a great place to put a favorite proverb into action. Proverbs 3:5-6 says, "Trust in the Lord with all of your heart and lean not on your own understanding. In all your ways acknowledge Him, and He will direct your path." As we trust the Lord to speak to us, we can continue to craft the treasure map of identity and the road map of destiny.

CHAPTER REFLECTIONS

What are some associations God is speaking through your name? Who are other people in the Bible, in history, in your circle of contemporaries, friends, and family members who share the same name? What qualities or virtues does that person possess that God is also highlighting in you?

_____

_____

_____

_____

Continue to craft the upgrades in identity for the names of three to five friends or family members you chose in chapter five reflections. What associations come to mind or heart with their names? Check in with Holy Spirit and write down your impressions.

_____

_____

_____

_____

There is no one like God; He is the ultimate standard, so every metaphor pales in comparison. However, that didn't stop Him from revealing Himself through parable language. Jesus said He was the door, the light of the world, the bread of Heaven, the good shepherd, and many other word associations. Choose one of these that Holy Spirit is highlighting to you and dig into what God is speaking about Himself through this comparison. Write your impressions below.

NAME ASSOCIATIONS

Chapter 8

Name Wordplays

Another heavenly tool that unlocks the power of your name is wordplay. Wordplay refers to the use of language in a witty or clever way to make a point. The Bible, including the teachings of Jesus, abounds with wordplay in the original languages of Hebrew, Greek, and Aramaic. One example found in the Old Testament is when God asked the prophet Jeremiah, "What do you see?" Jeremiah answered that he saw an almond branch. God affirmed to the prophet that what he saw was correct because, "... I'm watching over My word to perform it."[1]

> "It is perfectly logical to think that the Creator would communicate in creative ways."

Now, if we simply read this passage in an English translation, we will miss the connection. What does an almond branch have to do with God watching over His word? However, if we take a closer look at the original Hebrew words, we'll discover that God was using wordplay or a form of rhyme to convey a powerful prophetic message. He used the similarity in sound between the words *almond* (šāqēḏ) and *watching* (šāqaḏ) to deliver a profound word for the nation of Israel. The technique of wordplay unveiled a message from

God to the young developing prophet and serves as a beautiful example of how prophetic revelation can come through similar sounds in language.

There are some who may argue that God would not intentionally speak in this manner. We would propose that it is perfectly logical to think that the Creator would communicate in creative ways. The Bible uses multiple poetic forms and techniques to communicate spiritual truths, including acrostic, alliteration, allusion, anthropomorphism, apostrophe, assonance, chiasmus, hyperbole, idioms, imagery, merism, metaphor, metonymy, paradox, and many more. With all these creative expressions originating from the heart of God Himself, it should not surprise us that the Holy Spirit would also communicate through forms of rhyme and wordplay today.

GNATS AND CAMELS

Another example of wordplay in the New Testament is found in Jesus' admonition to the Pharisees in Matthew 23:23-24:

> Woe to you, scribes and Pharisees, hypocrites! For you tithe mint and dill and cumin and have neglected the weightier provisions of the law– justice and mercy and faithfulness; but these are the things you should have done without neglecting the others. You blind guides, who strain out a gnat and swallow a camel!

Why did Jesus compare a gnat and a camel? We understand that one is very small and the other big, but the Lord could have used any big or small comparison. A closer look at cultural history reveals that this statement is poking some poignant fun at the Pharisees using wordplay.

Historians tell us that the Pharisees would strain their beverages in case a gnat landed in them because, according to the strictest interpretation of Mosaic Law, a gnat in their drink would render them unclean. At the same time, there is the metaphoric picture of the Pharisees loading people down with laws and requirements like an overpacked camel[2] while they themselves did not address the weightier matters of justice, mercy, and faithfulness. All these cultural and biblical understandings factor into Jesus' meaning. Jesus often spoke and taught in Aramaic. but non-Aramaic readers would still miss a further power of the wordplay in their translations. In Aramaic, the word *gnat* is pronounced *galma* while the word *camel* in Aramaic is pronounced *gamla*. Jesus was using similar sounds to make His point meaningful and memorable.

This form of communication often occurs in the Bible regarding a person's name. Draw your attention again to Jacob's final blessings over his sons at the end of the Book of Genesis where he spoke to each of them using their names. When Jacob prophesied over his son Gad, he employed wordplay. Under the inspiration of the Holy Spirit, he said, "Gad will be attacked by a band of raiders, but he will attack them at their heels." The name *Gad* sounds like the Hebrew words for *attack* (gûd̠) and *band of raiders* (gᵊd̠ûd̠). It was a tongue-twister: gad—gûd̠—gᵊd̠ûd̠.

Throughout the Bible, the biblical authors often relayed God's message prophetically with similar sounds and wordplay; therefore, we know that it is one of the ways we can recognize His speaking today.

TERRY OR TARRY *(Dano)*

I remember one time a man introduced himself as Terry, and I immediately thought of the homophone *tarry* which means *to wait or linger with expectation.* The Holy Spirit then reminded me of Luke 24:49, "Tarry until you are endued with power from on high." I was able to share with Terry that God was pouring out a fresh boldness and power to witness upon his life. "That's exactly what I was praying for!" Terry exclaimed. Terry's response confirmed to me that God was speaking through the wordplay of similar sounds with different meanings.

Homophones, words that have the same pronunciation but are different in meaning or spelling, are not the only way God uses wordplay to reveal deeper insights. Let's revisit the example of Terry's name with a

> "God speaks through similar sounds."

hypothetical example of what this could look like. For instance, you might hear a completely different emphasis on the sounds or vowels in the name. Let's say you heard the word *teary*. The Holy Spirit might then link teary to Psalm 126:5, "Those who sow in tears shall reap in joy." Under the direction of the Holy Spirit, you might perceive that God is changing Terry's season from sowing to reaping and from sorrow to joy.

God speaks through similar sounds. The next time you think you may have misheard something, double-check to see if God may be speaking through wordplay.

THE DRANO ANOINTING *(Dano)*

During one of our training sessions in New Zealand, a senior leader heard my nickname as *Drano*. She perceived this as a word from the Lord and told me she felt the Lord was highlighting my anointing to *cut through blockages* and help people get *unstuck* like the drain cleaner brand called Drano unclogs plumbing. This simple wordplay formed a prophetic identity that I enjoy and draw strength from to this day.

BET ON ME *(Bethany)*

Someone once shared with me that they heard a wordplay on my name as *Bet-On-Me*. This person felt the Lord was saying that I was someone whom He trusted and was investing in or betting on.[3] He could trust the gifts and assignments He had given me because He knew I would carry them out. This deeply resonated with me. It was a creative and memorable way for the Lord to speak to the treasure of my heavenly identity through a wordplay on my name.

STANDING STAN *(Dano)*

As we shook hands, Stan's grip carried the force of a vice. His weathered hands and face spoke of the years of dues he had paid while working in the field under harsh conditions. When I heard his name, I also heard the word *stand*, along with the scripture from Ephesians, "after you have done everything to stand...stand firm then..."[4] By the Spirit, I perceived that Stan was on the verge of making a crucial decision and was tempted to give in to external pressure, but God was giving him the strength to stand his ground. I saw a flash vision of the Lord pouring steel and concrete into his back and midsection to make his resolve strong and his foundation sure. Stan later wrote to inform me that he was indeed in the middle of a business deal where all the voices around him were trying to get him to lower his price. He had been claiming the exact scripture I quoted over him. He stood his ground in a two-hundred-thousand-dollar business deal and won the account.

SOUNDS-LIKE FAMILY NAMES *(Dano)*

As with other prophetic tools, wordplay can also speak prophetically to last names. For instance, during a prophetic activation session a student heard my last name *McCollam* as the similar-sounding phrase *may call them*. From that similar sound, they prophesied that I had an anointing to call others to recognize and respond to the voice of God or to call them into God-encounters. I can attest to the fact that this is a primary passion and calling on my life that was confirmed through a similar sounding phrase.

When it comes to surnames, similar-sounding words may form the basis of prophetic encouragement not only for the intended receiver, but as a family name, it can also apply to the entire family line. While every prophetic impression should be confirmed through the conversation and leading of Holy Spirit, these impressions will often come and go at the speed of light. This requires quick recognition and a response of faith to grab hold of these flash impressions. Learning to pay close attention to the names of the people we meet will give us clues about prophetic encouragement that God wants to give them, often at a strategic time in their lives.

CHAPTER REFLECTIONS

What wordplay might be or has been associated with your first, middle, or last name? What might God be speaking to your identity and destiny through this wordplay? Write your impressions below.

_____
_____
_____
_____

Practice your wordplay tools on the names of family or friends you have been targeting for an upgraded heavenly identity. Write out word play connections for each of the three to five names you have chosen and ask Holy Spirit what He is revealing about their identity and destiny through these plays on words.

_____
_____
_____
_____

In this chapter, we stated that the Creator communicates in creative ways. God is a poet, a singer/songwriter, an artist, and a literary genius. He is a master communicator. Have you thought of God in this way before or is this a new idea to you? What do you think about God as a creative communicator who speaks to us today in creative ways? Write out your impressions.

CHAPTER END NOTES

1. Jeremiah 1:11-12.

2. Matthew 23:4

3. To bet on someone or something is to have a very strong hope that something will happen, so that this influences what you do. Accessed 6-4-2023.

4. Ephesians 6:13.

Chapter 9

Names of Places

Before we continue to unpack how our names prophetically speak to our personal identity and destiny, it's worth noting that the principles you've just learned in prophesying with names also apply to places. Just as individuals bear identity and purpose, so do places. The principle of the power in a name can reveal a place's identity which in turn affects its atmosphere and destiny. Let's explore some of the biblical basis connected to this topic of prophesying with the name of a place through our prophetic tools of name meaning, name association, and wordplay.

MEANING OF PLACE NAMES

When we hear the name of a place, we may think of its location, culture, or even its historical significance. Yet, there is a deeper layer to a place's name that can reveal its identity, atmosphere, and purpose.

In the Bible, names of places often carried prophetic significance. For example, the name *Bethel* means *house of God*. Jacob named this location Bethel since this is the place where he had a dream in which he saw a ladder reaching to Heaven and thus declared, "This is none other than the house of God and this is the gate of Heaven."[1]

The name *Jerusalem* means *city of peace*, and we are exhorted by the psalmist, "Pray for the peace of Jerusalem: 'May those who love you be secure.'"² While praying for peace is commendable for any city, this passage is strategic as the Lord invites us to pray in alignment with Jerusalem's true identity as a city of peace. The prayer is an affirmation of the name of the city and its ultimate destiny as a place of peace.

The significance of a place's name can also reveal its function and purpose. For instance, the name *Jericho* means *fragrant*, and it was a city known for its sweet-smelling spices and ointments.

The name *Galilee* means *circuit* or *district*, and it was a region that held a circuit of towns that bordered the Sea of Galilee.

The name *Bethsaida* means *house of fish*, and it was a small fishing village on the west shore of Lake Gennesaret. According to the Gospel of Luke, it was the location where Jesus performed the infamous miracle of feeding 5,000 with five loaves of bread and two fish.³

The name *Bethlehem* means *house of bread*, and it was the birthplace of Jesus who we celebrate as the Bread of Life.⁴

Are you catching the power in a name in these examples? By understanding the meaning behind a place's name, we can gain not only insight into its history and significance, but also recognize the work of God in its past, present, and future.

NAME ASSOCIATION FOR PLACES

What we have learned of associations regarding the appearances and names of people also applies to places. Two physical locations can carry a similar blessing or atmosphere that can be recognized or discerned through a prophetic association. You have likely been to a place that reminded you of somewhere else. These associations can be based on the fact that the two places have similar appearance or similar activity, but a connection of this type can also reveal a shared heavenly identity or purpose.

Why would we concern ourselves with prophetic impressions for places? Because as new creations, we are spiritual beings living in a physical world, and we have access to prophetic understanding that can open up a location's destiny, function, or atmosphere. Name association is one of the means that can provide the basis for this information.

> "As a new creation, you are a spiritual being living in a physical world."

For instance, many churches choose their name because of an association with an event that happened related to that name or the virtues associated with that name. If a church is named Zion Lutheran, they are associating with the biblical Mount Zion and the doctrine of Martin Luther. Bethesda Methodist is associating with the healing at the pool of Bethesda and John Wesley's Christian methodology. Both examples are identification through name association.

The same thing happens with the names of businesses, schools, and even cities. Over 1,700 cities in the world bear the name San Jose, which is associated with Jesus' earthly father, Joseph, the husband of the virgin Mary. Every city beginning with the prefix "San" is named from an association with the virtues of a historical or biblical saint.

SAN ANTONIO

A few years ago, we conducted prophetic training at a church in San Antonio, Texas. During one of the activations, we involved the attendees in a prophetic exercise which involves using spiritual gifts to locate missing items and individuals. The church's senior leader had recently lost an important journal that contained notes for a conference she was scheduled to speak at. They were in the process of moving, and the journal had been missing for about six weeks.

We activated the group by asking for insights and impressions from the Holy Spirit regarding what the missing item was as well as the item's whereabouts. About ten people were able to identify both that the missing item was a notebook and a range of similar descriptions of its location. The descriptions relayed of the various locations were not random guesses; instead, they appeared as subtle clues all pointing to the same destination.

Once we gathered and compared the prophetic intel, the journal owner's husband leapt up and hurried home to check the pinpointed location. He returned twenty minutes later, holding the journal in his hand. We all rejoiced in God's goodness for enabling us to locate this precious journal for the leader.

We have performed finding-lost-things exercises in several churches, cities, and countries, but San Antonio was by far the easiest place to identify both the missing item and its whereabouts. The San Antonio class demonstrated an above-average ability to locate items in many of our exercises. As we were commenting on their unusual grace for finding, someone from the audience stood up and said, "You know who San Antonio is named after?" He explained how the city was named after Saint Anthony, a Portuguese Roman Catholic priest who lived in the 1200s. Saint Anthony is recognized as the patron saint of lost things. Because San Antonio was named after Saint Anthony, it appears to have an anointing and grace for finding lost things. Prophetically speaking, the city of San Antonio carries in the spirit realm a similar atmosphere and anointing as the saint it is associated with.

Some people might dismiss this connection or write off the San Antonio example as coincidental. However, as we've seen both in the Bible and through experience, God speaks to real virtues, identities, and destinies through metaphoric associations. As sons and daughters of God, we hold a responsibility to pay attention to and, on occasion, actively seek out how God is speaking to the identity and destiny of cities through redemptive associations.

SAN FRANCISCO

For over two decades, our families have lived near the city of San Francisco. Prophets who had a negative focus were always predicting destruction over San Francisco because they only saw it as a city of sin. This is heartbreaking, not only due to the flawed theology but also because we love that city. What if people with prophetic tools used name association to better understand the holy virtues the city is called to. What does San Francisco look like through God's redemptive lens?

San Francisco, like San Antonio, was named after a saint. Saint Francis of Assisi, the son of an affluent 13th-century cloth merchant, chose to renounce his affluent lifestyle to minister to the poor and underprivileged.

There is, however, a strange paradox regarding this city. Although known for its cool and foggy weather, San Francisco has one of the top ten homeless populations in America. Why would the homeless choose to live in that city when a short walk across the bridge would provide nearly endless sunshine? Could it be that the homeless are being drawn on a deeper intuitive level that is based upon an unseen and unspoken connection to its association with its benevolent namesake?

Furthermore, could San Francisco's proclivity for environmental friendliness also be related to Saint Francis' love and connection with nature? What if we prophesied the identity and destiny of cities from their associated foundational virtues rather than their current problems and failures? What if we called them up rather than calling them out? Would cities rise to the virtue of their founding associations if they were called to remembrance? Are these the kind of redemptive aspects that people with prophetic gifts should be calling out? Since the nature of prophecy in the New Testament is to encourage, comfort, and strengthen, perhaps we should apply the same principles to how we see and speak about our cities, states, and nations.

WORDPLAY WITH NAMES OF PLACES

Lastly, the use of wordplay can reveal powerful prophetic identities found in the names of places. You can apply to places the same biblical basis and process of prophesying through wordplay as you would with a person's name.

Here are a few examples of wordplay with the city of Seattle, Washington. This city is often associated with rain and coffee, and one playful take on the city's name is *Sip-attle*, which nods to its famous coffee culture (think home of Starbucks). Another potential play on words is *Sea-addle*, referencing the city's maritime history and love for cycling.

Our current home is Austin, Texas. Name wordplays that come to mind as prophetic launchpads are *Awe-stonishing* or *Awesome*. This wordplay might reference the city's impressive music scene, natural beauty, or vibrant culture. Austin truly is an awe-stonishing city that the Father loves.

Each principle mentioned in this book regarding prophesying over a person's name also applies to places, cities, countries, businesses, street names, and more. The power in a name—its nature, virtues, identity, and destiny—is not exclusive to humans. It can be applied to any entity that has a name.

Scripture teaches us that Christ Jesus is reconciling all of creation back to God, and we are called to be ministers of this reconciliation. As ambassadors of Heaven, our responsibility is to prophetically call forth the identity and destiny of cities, regions, and nations. One way to do that is to view them through the redemptive lens of their names and in so doing, help them align with their heavenly identity. When using the power in a name, we are encouraged not only to bless people, but also to speak and call forth the blessings God has intended over places.

> "Our responsibility is to prophetically call forth the identity and destiny of cities, regions, and nations."

CHAPTER REFLECTIONS

Use the tools of name meaning, name association, and name wordplay to explore the virtues of the town or city where you currently live. What is God revealing about your city's identity and destiny through its name? Write a prayer of blessing for your city based on what Holy Spirit is revealing to you.

_____

_____

_____

_____

Choose a physical location that you would like to bless prophetically. Use the tools of name meanings and associations to have a dialogue with Holy Spirit about appropriate prophetic blessings to speak over this place. Write down your impressions below.

_____

_____

_____

_____

Heaven is a place. Use the tools of name meaning, name association, or wordplay to unlock some fresh revelations about it. Write your impressions below.

CHAPTER END NOTES

1. Genesis 28:10-19.

2. Psalm 122:6.

3. Luke 9:10-17.

4. John 6:35.

Chapter 10

Called by a New Name

While we have discovered that God speaks to our heavenly identity through our given names in the natural world, He also prophesies new names to us. Jacob the supplanter became Israel the prince.[1] Abram the exalted father became Abraham the father of a multitude.[2] These new names both announced and initiated a new or upgraded phase in the bearers' lives.

When Jesus wanted to change the way His disciples related and functioned with Him, He accomplished this by giving them a new name.

> No longer do I call you slaves, for the slave does not know what his master is doing; but I have called you friends, because all things that I have heard from My Father I have made known to you.
>
> John 15:15

This was a paradigm shift for the disciples. They had to choose to embrace a new way of seeing themselves so they could function and relate to Jesus appropriately. The called-out ones of Christ could no longer identify as slaves who did not understand the greater purpose of what the Lord was doing. These followers had to identify as friends of Christ so they could access the heart, will, and thoughts of the Father.

Let us emphasize that the initiation into this upgraded identity was given to the disciples in the form of a new name that Jesus spoke over them. The new name triggered the release of a new perspective. There are new names related to your heavenly identity and destiny that Jesus wants to reveal. These new names are not necessarily meant to replace your given name, but rather to complement it, revealing new layers of your spiritual identity and purpose.

> "There are new names related to your heavenly identity and destiny that Jesus wants to reveal."

SEEDS AND SEASONS

As God is both merciful and kind, most of us do not receive a complete download of all the ways that Heaven sees us at once. It would not be loving to reveal all that we are created to be in one moment; such a revelation could be overwhelming. Just as Jesus temporarily withheld many things He wanted to share with His disciples because they were not yet ready to bear them, God often speaks our identities to us as we are ready and willing to embrace them.[3] He often shares things in seed form and then watches how we steward the growth of each aspect of identity in our lives. Then, at the right time and season, He reveals a new name to upgrade how we see ourselves so that we can begin to step into a new destiny.

A TIMELY NEW NAME FOR ME *(Bethany)*

A few years ago, I participated in a question-and-answer panel session at School of the Prophets in Redding, California. After one of my answers elicited a standing ovation from the attendees, Kris Vallotton, the senior prophet of Bethel Church, stood and prophesied over me that I would "write the book that would redefine mothering in the kingdom of God." As he spoke those words, a new heavenly name was assigned to me as a kingdom mother. In that moment, I felt a mandate from the Lord that was assigned to this name settle in my spirit.

Two weeks later, while ministering with a team at a Baptist church in Texas, the senior leader turned towards me and said, "I have two words for you: Apostolic Mother!" I had not said anything to anyone about the original word in Redding, but the Lord was confirming my new identity and name through a second spiritual leader. Since that time, I have had several other prophetic words confirming and affirming this heavenly identity in my life.

FROM DRUNKARD TO WISE GUY *(Dano)*

In 1994, a spiritual renewal broke out across the earth. People stood in lines for hours to get a seat in churches where God was pouring out His Spirit. I had the privilege of being a worship leader and youth pastor in one of those churches. When God poured out His Spirit, I was locked into a previous belief system that revival could only come when I had prayed long and hard enough, fasted enough, and stood fully consecrated and surrendered to God. Yet, when God poured His Spirit out in this season, it seemed to be all about His grace and good intentions towards His people rather than a response to anything we had worked for. The kindness of God led people into repentance and a love connection with the Lord that was undeniable. We held services every night for six months and then slowed down to five nights a week for more than five years.

During this season I was so overwhelmed by the love and goodness of God that I would often just be lost in His presence. It was as if I was more conscious of the heavenly realm than of the earthly. I would easily be caught up in visions of glory or fall to the floor under the power of the Holy Spirit even in public places where it was at times embarrassing or inconvenient. Some people started identifying me as the town drunk in reference to Acts 2 where the disciples were thought to be drunk at the outpouring of the Holy Spirit on the Day of Pentecost. For seven years, I enjoyed this state of slipping in and out of the glory realm of God's love and presence.

Then, one day a prophet spoke over me. He said, "Dano, you have been known as the town drunk, but I saw the Lord crowning you with wisdom. You will be known as a man of wisdom." The next day, something changed in me. I still felt just as connected to the presence of the Lord, but I was much more tuned to what was going on around me. I began to have God-given insights and strategies for people, places, and organizations. People began to reference me as a man of wisdom just like the word through the prophet had said.

I had to learn in that transition to fully embrace my new season. I couldn't stay in the past or bemoan the change, I had to align myself with the new identity God had for me. It's been over twenty years since that change in identity marked a change of season and destiny. I truly believe that my season of exhilarating God-encounters was a detox from a wrong way of thinking that allowed me to come into and live in the power of a greater identity and destiny.

AN INVITATION TO SEE DIFFERENTLY

A new name is an invitation to upgrade how we see ourselves in light of something fresh that the Lord is revealing. It's not that He suddenly decides to call us something new; rather, in Heaven's eyes and in Christ, we have always been what He calls us. However, the divine timing of the revelation is strategic and relative to our readiness for that season in life. The wisdom of Proverbs reminds us that "a timely word is good."[4] In His goodness, God releases a new name at just the right time to initiate a new season of fullness in Christ Jesus.

> "God releases a new name at just the right time to initiate a new season of fullness in Christ Jesus."

Each one of us has new names that God is speaking over us. Likewise, places can also be called by new names. For example, the Lord spoke a new name over Jerusalem through Isaiah:

And you will be called by a new name, which the mouth of the Lord will designate. You will also be a crown of beauty in the hand of the Lord, and a royal headband in the hand of your God. It will no longer be said to you, "Forsaken," nor to your land will it any longer be said, "Desolate," but you will be called, "My delight is in her," and your land, "Married," For the Lord delights in you, and to Him your land will be married.

Isaiah 62:2-4

In this passage, the Lord gives the land a new name so it can step into the purpose and season God has hidden in His heart for it.

VACAVILLE'S NEW NAME *(Dano)*

A few decades ago, I lived in a city in Northern California that was struggling with gang problems. One of our youth pastors had even had his nose broken for inadvertently wearing the color of a rival gang in a local shopping mall. Something needed to change.

In that season, someone rented a billboard that boldly declared: "Vacaville, a place of peace." Many people scoffed at the idea since their experience of violence in Vacaville was contrary to a peaceful place. Our prayer warriors and prophetic community began to embrace the identity of this new name and come into agreement through prayer and faith. Today, the city has one of the lowest crime rates in the state and is truly a peaceful place to live. The prophetic declaration of a new name announced and released a new season for the entire city.

NEW NAMES IN HEAVEN

We will also receive new names in Heaven:

> To him who overcomes will be given... a new name written on the stone which no one knows but he who receives it.
>
> Revelations 2:17

There are new names that cannot be given until ages to come. It is possible that these new names will be necessary because we will have new functions and purposes on the other side of eternity.

New names represent the unfolding revelation of people and places moving from one level of glory to another with ever-increasing glory. Graham Cooke says it this way, *"Names are stepping stones into a new development of identity."*

Each of us has a multitude of names by which we are known: daughter, son, father, mother, pastor, employer, friend. Each of these names carries a corresponding responsibility and destiny. God reveals new names to unlock greater seasons for those who are ready. Seek the Lord for the new name that He is speaking over you.

CHAPTER REFLECTIONS

Think of a time when you received a new name, e.g., graduate, adult, husband, trainer, mother, etc. Consider how the new name shifted your view of self (identity) and your responsibilities (destiny). What new name does the Father want to call you by in this season, and what does it mean for you?

_____

_____

_____

_____

One of the great challenges of the ministry of reconciliation is to see people according to their spiritual potential rather than their current performance. Choose a person you know who is not living up to their full potential, and ask the Father how He sees them and what He calls them? Write out a crafted prayer according to who the Father says they are. Set your heart and mind to relate to them based upon this new view.

_____

_____

_____

_____

A new season also requires a new way of relating to God. Which of His names is God currently revealing to you? Who does the Lord want to be in you and for you in the season ahead?

_____

_____

_____

_____

CHAPTER END NOTES

---

1. Genesis 32:28.

2. Genesis 17:5.

3. John 16:12.

4. Proverbs 15:23.

Chapter 11

Your Heavenly Identity Statement

As we've explored the topic of the prophetic power of names in-depth, our hope is that you are becoming intrigued and attuned to the power in your own name.

In review, scripture provides a snapshot of the family traits you possess as a son or daughter in the family of God, also known as your spiritual last names. The meanings, associations, and wordplay of your earthly first, last, and middle names have prophetically illuminated hidden treasures of how God sees you. God-given new names announce new seasons and breakthroughs for you to walk in. Taken together, this information can help you understand and define your heavenly identity.

We understand that the amount of information we've provided can be overwhelming, making it challenging to mobilize or put into practice. To help harness the power of this knowledge, we have developed a method of condensing this information into a single biographical paragraph which we call your heavenly identity statement (HIS). In this chapter, we will guide you through the process of consolidating what you've learned in the previous chapters into a single, focused statement of your own heavenly identity.

We'll provide a sample worksheet on page 130 using Dano's identity statement workflow.

STEP ONE: GATHER

To create your heavenly identity statement, start by gathering all your identity information into one place.

The first question in the chapter reflections for chapters four, six, seven, eight, and ten were all crafted to help reveal secrets of your identity. If you didn't respond to those reflections in writing, now would be a good time to complete that assignment. In this step, we will make a bullet-point list of the things you discovered about yourself through these prophetic insights connected to your name.

From chapter four reflections, choose the names that most speak to you right now from the treasure of our family line in Christ as revealed in scripture. Though there are many treasures of identity to be unwrapped in scripture, try to choose two to four that most speak to you in this current season. Bullet point them below.

-
-
-
-

Next, drawing from your responses to chapter six reflections, list prophetic insights you gleaned from the meanings of your given name.

-
-

-

-

Then, drawing from your responses to chapter seven reflections, list the name associations you heard over your own name and the prophetic insights related.

-

-

-

-

Now list the wordplay associations you heard over your own name. Refer to your responses to chapter eight reflections for help.

-

-

-

-

Finally, add the information from your chapter ten new name reflections as bullet points.

-

-

-

DANO'S WORKSHEET

Kingdom Family Names

- chosen
- dearly loved
- faithful

Meanings From My Given Name

- Daniel - "judged of God"
- McCollam - "strong like a pillar"
- McCollam - "son of the dove"

Name Associasions

- Daniel in the Bible: a man of wisdom, a counselor to leaders, a revealer of mysteries
- Iron Man - innovative
-

Wordplay Using My Name

- drano - cuts through blockages, gets people unstuck
-
-

New Names

- a man of wisdom
- like David - raising up a mighty army to extend the Kingdom
-

STEP TWO: CRAFT YOUR PARAGRAPH

In the second step, you will craft these bullet point descriptions of yourself into a biographical paragraph called your heavenly identity statement or HIS. Imagine this paragraph to be like a brief two- to three-sentence description that would introduce you as an author on the back of a book or a short bio statement presenting you as a speaker on a conference advertisement.

Using the description examples, Dano's HIS might say:

> I am judged of God (name meaning for Daniel) to be faithful, chosen, and dearly loved (scripture identifications). I serve as a counselor to leaders and influencers by releasing wisdom and revealing mysteries (association with biblical Daniel) that help get them unstuck (wordplay with Drano). I am a builder of mighty ones who will extend God's kingdom in the earth (new names).

As you can see, this is a brief statement combining the descriptions of identity gathered from the reflection exercises in the previous chapters. It concisely describes how God sees you and how you should view yourself. Some of the statements may fit you well in this season, while others may challenge you or serve as catalysts to renew your way of thinking. Your HIS is like a lightning rod, pulling the power of your heavenly identity to earth where it can begin to shape who you are and why you are here.

> "Your heavenly identity statement is like a lightning rod, pulling the power of your heavenly identity to earth."

Use your bullet point statements to craft a single paragraph describing how God sees you. Begin your identity statement with "I am" to reinforce who you are rather than what you do.

I am:

_____

_____

_____

_____

THE TRUEST YOU

You may be questioning if these definitions are accurate descriptions of who you are now. Don't let that stop you. Your heavenly identity is the truest you. It is the revelation of the new creation you are in Christ Jesus. The Book of Ephesians tells us that not only did Christ die for us, but God also raised us up with Him and seated us in heavenly places in Christ Jesus. Think about it; while you are seated here on earth, you are also concurrently seated with Christ in heavenly places.

One theory of prophecy is that it reveals the person you already are as seated with Christ. Your heavenly man is finished and at rest, while your earthly man holds all the potential of your heavenly prototype. This tension between our heavenly identity and our earthly reality is why we sometimes feel a sense of frustration with our present and pressure to perform for our future. Throw off that pressure and live from the reality of what God has done in and for you. This identity is coming from Heaven to earth, so it may take a while for you to feel like it fits. Your heavenly identity encompasses the specific virtues of Jesus Christ within you. They are the expression of the unique fragrance of Christ you share with those around you.

UPGRADING IDENTITY

If your HIS doesn't challenge you, then you may benefit from redoing the reflection exercises in chapters four, six, seven, eight, and ten to upgrade your identity statement or to define a new season you may be ready for. According to the Bible, the sons and daughters of God are constantly changing and growing, going from glory to glory with ever-increasing glory.[1] There are times when you are growing so fast that last season's identity statement no longer challenges you. Be encouraged; the need for an updated identity statement is a clear sign that you are changing and maturing. It is time for a fresh revelation of how God sees you and time to create a new statement with these same prophetic tools. It could also be that you simply need to keep refining your current identity statement until it carries the weight of a heavenly view. Remember, though, it is important to keep your HIS brief enough to memorize.

While understanding and embracing your heavenly identity is a vital first step, knowing and understanding what to do with it offers your next growth opportunity. In the next chapter, we will show you very practical ways that your identity statement can shape your thinking, your behavior, and your destiny.

> "There are times when you are growing so fast that last season's identity statement no longer challenges you."

CHAPTER REFLECTIONS

What part or parts of your identity statement are most difficult for you to believe and why? What statements are most compelling and why?

_____

_____

_____

_____

You can use the same tools to craft a heavenly identity statement over a friend, family member, or client. How would seeing a person from God's view of them shape how you relate to them?

_____

_____

_____

_____

Each chapter reflection in this book contains a focus on God's identity. Collect the information from your God reflections in the previous chapters and use the space below to craft a statement of how God wants you to see Him in this season.

_____

_____

_____

_____

CHAPTER END NOTES

1. 2 Corinthians 3:18.

Chapter 12

Owning Your Name

Now that you know who God says you are, you possess the power to see yourself differently. What will you do with this newfound knowledge?

Start by agreeing with it—not merely a mental acknowledgement but a deep, core-level agreement with who God says you are. Have faith in His words and trust what He has spoken about you. Your identity statement is an expression of Christ in you. Walking out and living from your heavenly identity is one of the most profound expressions of faith. Remember, who God says you are is the truest thing about you in the universe. The question is will you choose to believe it?

God's thoughts about you are brilliantly beyond anything you could ask, think, or even imagine. However, many Christians tend to dismiss or disqualify God's perception of themselves simply because they do not see it as their current reality. Living at a God-sized level of awesomeness seems impossible to picture. The challenge we all face is learning to agree with and live from His truth rather than resorting to or returning to the lies we have believed our entire lives.

THE NATURE OF FAITH

Agreement is an issue of faith. Let's take a moment to define this important word as it applies to your heavenly identity. Faith is not just about what we believe but also about how we believe and what we do with those beliefs. James, the half-brother of Jesus, emphasized this reality when he wrote, "In the same way, faith also, if it has no works, is dead, being by itself."[1]

When faith exists only in our minds as a concept, it is merely a hazy illusion of a spiritual reality. It lacks life and substance until it is put into practice. The substance of faith requires an equal action of living from that belief. In our context, this is owning your name! You are not just believing what God says as mere information or head knowledge; rather, you are embracing every ounce of favor, identity, and authority that God associates with that name and putting it into practice.

When we believe who God says we are and live out of that identity, we displace every lesser voice and shine like new creations. The new creation of Christ in you makes this all possible. Putting feet to our belief systems by owning who He says we are—regardless of how we appear to others or feel within ourselves—demonstrates the kind of faith that scripture tells us pleases God.[2] We learn to trust that what God says is truer than how we feel in the moment and put our faith in His words above our own.

Believing and acting on who He says we are is a powerful expression of faith. In fact, it takes more faith to live as a son and daughter of God than as a servant because a servant only does what their master tells them. There's no risk involved as the servant has no responsibility outside of doing what they are instructed to do. It takes faith to operate as His child because we don't always have a step-by-step plan as a servant would. Sons and daughters live by permission, and the Lord loves to see how His children choose to reveal His ways and kingdom in the earth. Whenever we operate this way and manifest our heavenly identity, we walk in faith. We choose His voice above every other voice and act on it. Pastor Bill Johnson in Redding, California, beautifully says it this way, "You can't afford to have one thought in your head that God doesn't think about you."

> "What names you believe and declare about yourself will shape your reality."

It has been said that our words create worlds, implying that humans shape the world around them according to the words they believe within. What names you believe and declare about yourself will shape your reality. Partnering with the original and ultimate Creator who spoke the universe into existence with His words is the wisest choice for shaping your world.

KNOWING AND BELIEVING

Owning your heavenly identity mirrors the biblical concept of knowing and believing. In the first letter of John to the church he writes,

> We have come to know and have believed the love which God has for us. God is love, and the one who remains in love remains in God, and God remains in him.
>
> 1 John 4:16

When we believe something, it sets us up to experience it. By acting on that faith, we gain experience, and that experience leads to a more solid surety. This is why John links knowing and believing in God's love with the ability to stay or remain within it. By moving from mere believing to experiential knowing, we gain an anchored position of faith. The great revivalist Leonard Ravenhill wrote, "A man with an experience of God is never at the mercy of a man with an argument."

The same is true of knowing who you are in Christ. When we take action based on our faith and gain experience from it, it transforms us from simply believing into actually knowing. At that point, we become firm and unwavering in our position. Our internal doubts and external voices are silenced by our conviction of the truth that God has spoken. Like the biblical writer John, we can declare, "We have come to know and have believed," and remain anchored in the realities of that truth. This is what it means to own your name.

OWN IT! *(Bethany)*

People often comment on my confidence, but few may understand that it comes from my conviction in who God is and who He has named me to be. Whenever I step into a room or onto a platform feeling disqualified, unanointed, or insecure, I remind my soul of who God says I am. I rehearse a portion of my heavenly identity to myself that says, "I am a prophet whose words shift atmospheres. I am a Deborah anointed to break false mindsets. I am a faith-releasing kingdom bringer, and I am the perfect woman for the job!"

I put on my heavenly identity like a coat and step confidently into any situation, knowing that who God says I am is far superior to anything I may lack. These statements are not just positive affirmations that make me feel good. I don't stand in front of a mirror trying to pump up my self-image with meaningless flattery. The words represent my truest identity declared over me by God Himself. They are in one sense His words becoming flesh. When I remind myself of them, I feel the weight of Heaven's force and approval. As I go to the places He has called me, I don't have to strive to be someone I'm not. Instead, I simply lean on God's voice of identity and affirmation and the reality of Christ in me. I remind myself that I am a Kingdom bringer, a faith releaser, and that my words can shift atmospheres. With this faith-charged reminder, I show up and simply be myself.

Our heavenly identity is a powerful expression of faith that reveals truth about ourselves that surpasses our own understanding. However, to fully experience the power of a name, we need to take ownership of it through a deep level of agreement. This requires embracing who God says we are with our whole hearts and rejecting any beliefs that conflict with this truth. By taking firm hold of God's truth, we displace and overcome any negative beliefs that have held us back in the past, and we tap into the incredible power that comes from living in the fullness of who God created us to be. Let us confidently embrace our identity as God sees us and boldly step into the destiny He has prepared for us.

CHAPTER REFLECTIONS

What is your current level of agreement with who God says you are and why?

_____

_____

_____

_____

What are the obstacles you face in seeing others the way that God sees them, and how will you overcome them?

_____

_____

_____

_____

Every time you believe who God wants to be to you, you access that part of His nature. Journal a time when believing in who God said He was resulted in your experiencing that part of His nature.

_____

_____

_____

_____

CHAPTER END NOTES

1. James 2:17.

2. Hebrews 11:6.

Chapter 13

Warring with Your Name

In the last chapter, we discussed the importance of agreeing with our heavenly identity. Agreement, however, is only the first step in experiencing the full power and blessing of this revelation. In this chapter, we will explore how to align our internal beliefs and behaviors with who God says we are.

As we deepen our understanding of what God is revealing through our natural and spiritual names, we enter a new phase of spiritual warfare. Every transformational truth will be challenged by the enemy of our souls. The apostle Paul told his spiritual son Timothy that by recalling the prophetic words he had received, he would be enabled to fight well.

> Timothy, my son, I am giving you this command in keeping with the prophecies once made about you, so that by recalling them you may fight the battle well.
>
> I Timothy 1:18

We war from who God says we are. This warring *from* is an important distinction. Many people receive a revelation of their heavenly identity and then try to live towards it with human effort and striving as if they were responsible for forming themselves into

> "We war from who God says we are."

a new creation. This represents a wrong understanding of spiritual warfare. You are not warring with yourself; you are warring against the demonic lies that have tried to limit and redefine you. Your prophetic identity is a result of the new creation that emerged when you were born again; it is not something of human origin. You live from this reality not toward it.

We wage war with a spiritual foe by words and beliefs inspired by the Chief of Spirits, the Lord of Hosts. Therefore, the next step in warring with your heavenly identity is internal alignment. Alignment refers to arranging things in a correct or appropriate relative position. If seated in Christ in heavenly places is our correct and appropriate relative position, then what should our internal beliefs and behaviors look like?

DISPLACEMENT WARFARE

Alignment in fighting the good fight—as the New American Standard Bible phrases 1 Timothy 1:18—pertains to what we do with what we believe about ourselves. It involves how we will personally steward those heavenly truths. The author Graham Cooke says, "The strongest form of warfare is displacement." You can't simply say no to a lie and expect things to change. When you cut off an inferior belief or behavior, it creates a void. That void becomes a battleground for occupation. You must occupy the space that the lie took up with a truth or virtue or it will be invaded again by dark forces. This occupation is displacement warfare. Let's look at how the Bible describes this type of warfare in a simple principle: "Do not be overcome by evil; but overcome evil with good."[1]

Do you see the displacement here? The way to not be overcome by evil is to overcome evil with good. The same is true with our heavenly identities. Knowing who you are as a new creation in Christ Jesus empowers you to displace both the internal and external lies you have believed so that you can resist the enemy. The truth of your heavenly identity occupies the space that the lie took up and becomes your weapon for fighting the good fight.

> "You can't do what God says you will do until you believe you are who God says you are."

To illustrate this point, let's revisit the story of Gideon. When the Angel of the Lord called Gideon a mighty warrior even though he was hiding out in a winepress threshing wheat, Gideon had a choice to make. Initially, he argued with the angel, essentially stating that Heaven picked the wrong guy since he was the youngest and least significant in his clan. But the angel's declaration of a new identity is Gideon's opportunity for transformation. Would he continue to believe the devilish lie that he is simply too small and weak to defeat his nation's powerful foe, or will he rise in holy confidence in his heavenly identity and take his place as Israel's champion? Before the battle can be won on the outside, the mental and spiritual ground must be taken on the inside. The internal impacts the external because the kingdom of God is within us, and our mandate is to manifest that Kingdom on the earth.

You can't do what God says you will do until you believe you are who God says you are. That doesn't mean that you act arrogantly and self-importantly. No, you humbly embrace the treasure of your heavenly identity and learn to live out that revelation in your earthly reality. Every single person on this planet must learn to overcome demonic lies and displace them with the truth of who they are in Heaven's eyes.

THE EXAMPLE OF JESUS

Jesus fought the good fight of faith with His heavenly identity. At the river Jordan, the Holy Spirit descended from Heaven in the form of a dove, and the voice of the heavenly Father said, "This is My Beloved Son in whom I am well-pleased." Immediately after this triumphant revelation, the Spirit led Jesus into the wilderness and into a bout of warfare. A transformational truth will always be field tested. At the end of a forty-day fast, the enemy came to challenge Jesus on the truth of His identity. The first temptation thrown at Him was, "If You are the Son of God, command that these stones become bread."[2]

The temptation was to create bread to satisfy His hunger, but the challenge was to His heavenly identity. The enemy was trying to entice Jesus to prove through performance what He already had by relationship and by the declared word of the Lord. The battle was over what Jesus believed about Himself and what His motives would be for displaying that identity. Jesus answered this challenge with the classic quote of Deuteronomy 8:3, "Man shall not live by bread alone, but by every word that proceeds from the mouth of God." This verse is often quoted as if it is talking about the power of scripture in warfare. While Jesus did use scripture to fight when He said, "It is written...," the phrase "every word that proceeds from the mouth of God" is referring here to the word the Father had prophetically spoken to Him at His baptism. Jesus was in effect saying, "I just heard my Father say that I am His Son and that He is already pleased with me; I don't have to labor to prove it to you."

The devil will always attack who you are and try to convince you that you are not enough or that you must perform harder to prove who you are.

Don't fall for it. Resolve in your heart and mind the truth that God has spoken over you, and rest in it.

ATMOSPHERE CHANGER *(Dano)*

In my forties, I received a personal prophetic word where God called me *atmosphere changer* and *culture creator*. Growing up, I was very sensitive to atmospheres and my environment. Later in life, as a trainer and speaker who traveled from city to city, I often discerned dark or negative activity in the atmosphere. In those meetings, my effectiveness would be greatly limited. I reasoned that my limited effectiveness was because of spiritual warfare or sin blockages in the atmosphere. I reasoned that it wasn't my fault, it must be this church or this city's problem. However, after enduring many years of less powerful meetings, the Holy Spirit revealed to me that my acquiescing to the negative activity in the atmosphere was actually a form of agreement which further empowered it. I was living my life outside-in and choosing to become a victim of my environment. But when God called me *atmosphere changer* and *culture creator*, I had to reject the victim mentality, embrace this identity, and learn to live from the inside-out. Instead of allowing the atmosphere to impact me, I now understood that I had been sent to change the atmosphere.

This decision and conviction of internal alignment with my heavenly identity and the authority, favor, and influence attached to who God said I was had a transformative external effect. Since that discovery, I rarely feel or prove ineffective as I travel to minister. Knowing who I was in Christ was not enough; I had to apply the authority of that identity to every situation. Remember, the word you carry within you will affect the world you create around you.

EXTERNAL ALIGNMENT

External alignment refers to taking actions to prepare yourself as much as possible for what God has promised. It's easy to get discouraged with the distance between our prophetic promises and their fulfillment. We can easily sit around questioning why God's promises take so long to come. The prophet Habakkuk wrote about this when he said, "For the revelation awaits an appointed time; it speaks of the end and will not prove false. Though it linger, wait for it; it will certainly come and will not delay."[3]

There is a definite paradox presented here. Though it lingers, it will not delay. And here is an even greater mystery: the promise can't be delayed because it is already a heavenly reality. It wasn't something that had to be proven or become, yet it did need to be believed and lived out. God speaks from end to beginning because He wants us to live from Heaven's finished work rather than towards the vanity and futility of mere human achievement. When we start at the end, we live like heavenly citizens, and God receives the glory for who we are and what is accomplished.

THE GREAT DISTANCE

From this vantage point, understand that frustration in waiting for a future promise is more than impatience; it is a form of ignorance. The distance between the promise made and its fulfillment is a gift of time, allowing for personal growth and development that would ultimately work toward sustainable victory. My friend Kris Vallotton says something like this, "If you enter a palace thinking like a pauper, you will turn the palace into a prison of poverty because you will create the reality around you that you carry within you." In the process of time, God is giving you room to align your thinking with Heaven and to war against opposing realities.

This is where external alignment comes into play. Alignment can be an accelerant to prophetic promise. God speaks a promise to mark the course and then gives us time to align ourselves with Heaven for a sustainable victory. As you walk out the treasure map of who Heaven says you are, you find your pleasurable pathway of purpose. Here is a personal example to illustrate this point.

CALLED TO PREACH *(Dano)*

I knew that I was called to preach at six years old even though I wasn't yet born again and had no idea what preaching was. After my salvation at fourteen, I toured with various Christian and marketplace bands until I was twenty-three. In these concerts, I would often share a short salvation message, and over the years, we saw thousands of people come to Christ. However, I still felt a deep longing to preach the Word and invest my life more fully into a group of people.

One day, while still on tour with the band, I cried out to God, "Lord, why don't I have invitations to preach?" His response shocked me. He asked, "Well, what would you preach if you had an opportunity today?" Besides my regular call for salvation, I had no preaching topics prepared and no idea what I would say. Challenged, I immediately sat down with my Bible and pen and spent hours hammering out a message.

The next day, I presented my sermon pages before the Lord and said, "Here it is, Lord! This is what I would preach!" But God's response was unexpected yet again. He said, "That is yesterday's manna. What would you preach today?" So, I spent hours preparing another message. This happened every day. For 365 days, I prepared a fresh message each day as if I had to preach it that night.

On the 366th day, I received a phone call from my former youth pastor asking me to speak to his group of 250 youth. I accepted the invitation, and we had a powerful meeting where teens and parents flooded the altars for an extended period. Word of that meeting got out and led to my being invited to be a full-time vocational youth pastor. I left the touring band life and settled in as a vocational minister, preaching and teaching every week.

Do you see the gift of time? The distance between the call or promise and the fulfillment was a gift of time for my personal development. I had to align myself in preparation for a more sustainable victory. I didn't create the call or identity of *preacher*; that came from Heaven, but I did prepare myself by appropriately aligning with the skills needed to be who God called me to be.

When we come into a promise unprepared in terms of

our character, skills, resources, and relationships, we may experience a momentary victory, but it will likely not last long term. External alignment, then, can be described as the actions you take to the best of your ability to prepare yourself for what God has promised.

PREPARING FOR NATIONS *(Dano)*

Here is another personal example of preparing myself for a promise.

I received a word from the Father many years ago that I would impact nations. When I asked the Holy Spirit which nations I would go to, He answered, "I will not send you to any nation you haven't prayed for."

At the time, I was working as a youth pastor with a severely limited income. However, with my wife's permission, I invested $75 in a pictorial atlas of the world. This large coffee-table book featured two pages of pictures, maps, and vital statistics for every country in the world.

Each day, I would open those giant pages and learn about a new country by studying the pictures, maps, and topography and reading information presented about that nation's religion, languages, economy, and more. At every turn of the page, I asked the Holy Spirit, "If I were standing in this nation or in front of its leaders today, what would I say? How would I pray? What would I prophesy?" For a year and a half, I prayed over every nation in the world multiple times until God opened the doors.

When He first called me to impact nations, I couldn't afford to go and had no invitations. However, by the time the door to the nations opened, my faith and finances were in a better place for a sustainable victory.

THE GIFT OF DEVELOPMENT

If you have ever resented the distance between your promises and their fulfillment, we want to encourage you to renew your mind. The gap between who God says you are now and fully owning the benefits of your name is a gift of development that leads to a sustainable victory. Cherish the time like a gift. Welcome it as a friend. Steward it with precious care and wisdom.

To fight the good fight with your prophetic names and words, ask yourself, "What can I do now to prepare myself better for walking in the fullness of who God says I am and what He says I will do?" Recognize whether your battle is mainly internal or external. Examine yourself for thoughts and restricting boxes that need to go and ask the Holy Spirit for the truths that can displace them. What external behaviors are currently out of alignment with who Heaven says you are? What steps can you take to prepare yourself for a more sustainable future victory? The answers to these questions paired with your heavenly identity will empower you to fight the good fight and win!

CHAPTER REFLECTIONS

Which area(s) of personal development could you give yourself to right now that might lead to a more sustainable future victory in the area of your calling? Dialogue with Holy Spirt on at least three practical steps to align yourself with who God says that you are. Write them below.

_____

_____

_____

_____

Many people dismiss their responsibility to the fulfillment of a future promise by saying they are "waiting on God." From what you have learned in this chapter, what counsel would you give them?

_____

_____

_____

_____

If you have ever resented the distance between your promise and its fulfillment, take a moment to repent. Write a prayer of repentance and thanksgiving for the gift of developmental time to the Lord in the space below:

_____

_____

_____

_____

CHAPTER END NOTES

1. Romans 12:21.

2. Matthew 4:3.

3. Habakkuk 2:3.

Chapter 14

Living from Heavenly Authority

Once you have won the internal ground by agreeing and aligning yourself with your heavenly identity, it is time to take appropriate steps forward. So far, what you have studied and put into practice has been about transforming yourself; now it's time to externalize the power of your name to transform the world around you.

There is authority, favor, and influence attached to every piece of your heavenly identity. If God calls you *bold,* then you can take your next step with confidence. If God calls you *industrious,* then you can roll up your sleeves and persevere. If God calls you *creative,* then it is time to press through barriers and release your creativity to the world. You may not be able to do everything God says you will do in this moment, but you can certainly begin to act with the authority, favor, and influence of who God says you are and move in the direction of your compelling purpose.

KINGS AND THRONES

David is the most celebrated king in Israel's history, yet he didn't need a throne to act like a king. He received the revelation of his heavenly identity from the prophet Samuel at a party to which he wasn't even invited. When the prophet realized that God's chosen one was not there, the servants had to go fetch David from the fields. David was anointed king in the sight of his brothers, but there was still a long journey to the throne.[1]

It would be fourteen years between the heavenly revelation and the earthly recognition of David's kingship. Yet, during that waiting period David did everything a king would do without a throne. Scripture tells us how he defended and expanded Israel's borders, overcame its enemies, built one of the greatest armies on earth in a desert with no budget, and counseled and conferred with kings. David did all these kingly things before he ever wore a crown. Embracing the truth of his heavenly identity, he took appropriate outward steps according to who God said he was. By the time of his coronation, he was the obvious choice to everyone.

Don't wait for the stars and planets to align before you step out. You are not waiting on Heaven; Heaven is waiting on you! There is something appropriate you can do now.

Many years ago, the prophet Graham Cooke led our church through a spiritual visualization exercise. The group had all crafted heavenly identity statements and studied Ephesians 2:6 which reveals that believers are raised up with Christ and are seated in heavenly places in Christ Jesus. We each read through our heavenly identity statements, and then Graham asked us to visualize ourselves seated in Christ Jesus. He encouraged us to envision ourselves as finished works in Christ as described by our identity statements. He asked, "What do you feel? Do you feel strong, confident, peaceful, and assured? If that's what you're like while seated in heavenly places in Christ, then why not act like that right now and right here from that position?" This exercise makes the second line of the Lord's Prayer very personal. Instead of praying, "May it be on earth as it is in Heaven," dare to pray, "May I be on earth as I am in Heaven!" It's a bold act of prayer, but if we believe the scriptures that speak of us being raised with and seated in Christ in heavenly places, then we must appropriate that reality to be a blessing to the world around us.

MORE THAN YOU HAVE BECOME

There is a classic line in the Disney movie *The Lion King* that speaks to this point. In the story, the young heir to the throne loses his wise and regal father in a tragic accident. Blaming himself for the death, the young lion runs away, abandoning the lion pride and leaving the throne to the occupation of an evil uncle. In a far-off land, the young lion lives a careless and playful existence until a spiritual vision of his father speaks to him, "Simba, you are more than you have become." It's a turning point for Simba and one for us as well. Simba returns to his pride to drive out the evil and retake the throne.

Through the redemption of Christ and as His new creation, we are each more than we have become. We are sons and daughters of the King, yet we often allow evil to rule while we live playfully and carelessly. But, when you take hold of your heavenly identity, you remember who you truly are and your commission to displace evil in the world around you with the kingdom of God.

> "Through the redemption of Christ and as His new creation, we are each more than we have become."

PRESENT OR FUTURE?

While God's promises are frequently fulfilled in the future, our heavenly identity is meant to be experienced and expressed in the present. We have the ability to embrace our heavenly identity here and now, in this lifetime. The virtues associated with our heavenly identity are a present reality as we have already been raised up with Christ. You are currently seated with Him in heavenly places. This position makes the authority, favor, and influence of your heavenly identity available to you now; it's not just a benefit that pays out when you die. Do not delay experiencing your greatest blessings until eternity when they are available to you now. Appropriate your new creation here on earth as it is in Heaven.

From this heavenly position, we can act like the kings and queens we are even if we have not yet come into the earthly "throne" of promise. Remember that you are no longer defined by the earth's method of judging value: You are because you have done. Now you live by the heavenly performance standard: You do because you are. Choose to adopt this higher heavenly way of thinking about yourself. Act from the authority of who Heaven says you are.

STAYING HUMBLE

One of the great concerns we are often challenged with when presenting these ideas is the fear of pride. People are concerned that they might become proud if they believe and behave with such boldness. We would answer them by saying that pride is thinking more of yourself than what is true. You won't become proud by embracing God's truth. Don't mistake confidence for arrogance. Prophecy is meant to encourage and strengthen, so it should make you courageous and strong.

A greater plague than overt pride in the Body of Christ is the scourge of false humility. In the name of trying to stay humble, believers tend to see themselves as less: "I'm a worm. I am nothing." They speak these things as if declaring themselves to be less somehow makes them more righteous. This may sound like spiritual humility, but it is simply the fear of pride. These belittling descriptions demonstrate what we were before being born again, but they do not adequately describe the glories of the new creation we are in Christ Jesus.

Fear is faith in the wrong kingdom. Whatever you have faith in, you will attract. Fear of pride will not repel pride; it will attract it. Pride is thinking that you know better than God. Living less than who God says you are, cannot be anything but tragic. If God says you are mighty, and you say you are nothing, are you not saying you know better than God? To diminish your identity as sons and daughters of God in the name of humility is an act of rebellion against the throne of God. If you are nothing special, then you are not to blame for the state of the world; but if you are the light of the world, the ambassador of God, a minister of reconciliation, then shoulder your responsibility and act like it by appropriating your heavenly identity.

It's important to remember that God's perspective is so much higher than ours,[2] and we should trust that He knows what He's doing when He names us. By embracing the names that God has given us, we can walk confidently in our true identity and fulfill the purposes He has for us.

WHO IS CHEERING FOR YOU?

Let's talk about your support group in this new way of seeing yourself. Parents are usually great at attending their kids' sporting events, award ceremonies, and performances. It's very empowering to see someone you love in the stands cheering for you. We are deeply sorry if you have never experienced this but want to encourage you that you can experience it now. We quoted the second half of a verse earlier in this book regarding throwing off entanglements, but let's look at the first part of the verse which reveals our motive and support.

> Therefore, since we are surrounded by such a great cloud of witnesses, let us throw off everything that hinders, and the sin that so easily entangles. And let us run with perseverance the race marked out for us.
>
> Hebrews 12:1

Heaven's heroes have not only run as our examples, but they are now the great cloud of witnesses who are cheering on the runners who now hold the baton—that includes you. Run the race that is marked out for you. That race is marked by who God created you to be which is found in the names He calls you. Be fully who God says you are, and then run the race. Persevere and don't give up.

Creation is also cheering for you. Well, maybe it's more like groaning. Paul's letter to the Roman church says that all of creation has been groaning and travailing, waiting for the sons and daughters of God to be revealed.[3] Like C.S. Lewis' classic novel series, *The Chronicles of Narnia*, the created realm is waiting for the sons of Adam and the daughters of Eve to liberate it from the frustrations and limitations that human depravity had placed upon it. Creation is crying out for your life as a son or daughter of God to make a difference in this world.

The revelation of who you are in Christ creates a weight of glory. You might be thinking right now, "Wow, that's a lot of pressure! Heaven and earth are counting on me?" While we affirm that there is great responsibility associated with who you are in Christ Jesus, the yoke of Jesus is easy, and His burden is light.[4] We are not pressuring you to take giant

> "Be fully who God says you are, and then run the race."

leaps forward but to at least take baby steps in the direction of who God has called you to be. Even as you are gathering courage and confidence, you can take a step that makes a small amount of progress toward achieving your purpose.

BABY STEPS

What do we mean by baby steps? One of our pastors often joked that the best study on pastoring was the comedy movie *What About Bob?* He was referring to the suffocating dependence that some people have on their pastor in their journey towards wholeness. If you've seen the movie, you get it. In the film, Marvin, the psychologist, gives his phobia-filled client Bob a copy of his brand-new book called *Baby Steps*. Marvin encourages Bob to set small, reasonable goals for himself: "One day at a time, one tiny step at a time—a doable, accomplishable goal."

The movie is funny, but the concept is real. Small, achievable goals in the direction of your heavenly person are the keys to fighting the good fight. Discovering the many ways to act out the power of your name in real life will make the appropriation of it fun and achievable.

Remember the personal testimonies shared earlier. Writing one sermon a day with no invitations to preach—that was a baby step in the direction of calling. Praying each day for a nation of the world prior to any opportunity or invitation to go—that was a baby step in the direction of desire. When Gideon accepted his heavenly identity and tore down his father's altar to a false god, that was a baby step. Later Gideon would face massive armies, but first he needed to take incremental steps of faith in the direction of his ultimate call.

You are royal priests. You are sons and daughters of the Most High God. You are new creations in Christ Jesus. You are the light of the world. Now you understand how your name holds the secrets of the treasure map to your identity and the road map to your destiny. Choose to believe, align, and appropriate who Heaven says you are and watch the world around you change under the power of Christ revealed in and through you.

CHAPTER REFLECTIONS

What is an outward step you could take to appropriate the power of your name and heavenly identity?

_____
_____
_____
_____

Choose a friend or family member who you have done some reflection work over in previous chapters. What steps could they take to appropriate the power of their name? How might you encourage them with these revelations?

_____
_____
_____
_____

As sons and daughters of God, we can also appropriate the power of His name. Because He is Savior, we can offer salvation. Because He is Healer, we can minister healing. What is a name of God that you have not yet appropriated the power of, and what would it look like to do so?

_____
_____
_____
_____

CHAPTER END NOTES

---

1. 1 Samuel 16:12-13.

2. Isaiah 55:9.

3. Romans 8:22.

4. Matthew 11:30.

Chapter 15

Heavenly Identity Shapes Culture

Heavenly identity also shapes how we do community. As you have been reading through this book, you have been presented with chapter reflections. The first reflection in each chapter speaks to your view of yourself. The second chapter reflection has been about how you see the people around you. Your heavenly lens not only allows you to serve and add value to the people around you, but it also empowers you to see them differently. Heaven's redemptive lens becomes our way of viewing the rest of humanity. This is how God wants us to view one another. Paul affirmed this truth by saying,

> So, from now on we regard no one from a worldly point of view. Though we once regarded Christ in this way, we do so no longer. Therefore, if anyone is in Christ, the new creation has come; the old has gone, the new is here!
>
> 2 Corinthians 5:16-17

Paul's description reminds us how the disciples at one time only saw Jesus by His earthly performance. He was considered the son of a carpenter, a great teacher, a prophet who worked miracles. These external observations or names comprised the disciples' earthly assessments of Jesus' identity. But once His followers saw Jesus as the Christ, the Son of the Living God, they were introduced to a whole new way of seeing Him and one another. Once your eyes have seen from a heavenly perspective, you long for more. What would a church be like if its members saw each other through lenses of heavenly identity? How would we regard one another? What would a city be like? How would this heavenly view shift modern culture?

> "As a new creation culture, we cannot afford to view one another in an old and earthly way."

Some believers live solely with the goal of reaching Heaven. Their earthly lives are governed by certain rules and principles as they try to be and do good until the kingdom of Heaven comes to them through death. However, new birth in Christ Jesus has made it possible for each of us to live from the heavenly realm now. The Bible teaches that the old has gone and the new has already come.[1] As new creations, we have not only been given a personal new start, but we have also been presented with a lens through which we can see one another as Heaven does. As a new creation culture, we cannot afford to view one another in an old and earthly way.

A NEW ACCOUNTABILITY

What would this heavenly lens change? One of the cultural shifts enabled by a heavenly lens is a new way to view accountability. Growing up in the church, accountability was often described as holding another to the basic Christian standards of behavior. Unfortunately, this type of accountability often represented the lowest expectation of proper performance. Accountability interviews typically included, "Have you smoked, gotten drunk, or done drugs? Have you lied, deceived anyone, or cheated on your taxes? Have you been pure in your heart and faithful to your spouse?" While these questions certainly have value, they presume a disposition toward failure and sin. This view conditions the average believer with more faith for failure and sin than for freedom and victory. This tragic view exists whenever we focus on earthly possibilities rather than heavenly. What if sinful behaviors are just a vision problem? Consider the wisdom of Proverbs 29:18, "Where there is no revelation, people cast off restraint; but blessed is the one who heeds wisdom's instruction."

Could it be that the behavioral lack of restraint is connected to the absence of compelling heavenly revelation? People don't heed wise instruction because they live without personal spiritual revelation. Having a clear spiritual vision is directly related to having self-control. How well you can govern yourself depends on the level of your aspirations and ambitions. Paul uses the metaphor of an Olympic runner to explain how vision governs behavior: "Everyone who competes in the games goes into strict training. They do it to get a crown that will not last, but we do it to get a crown that will last forever."[2]

Runners modify their own behavior, restricting themselves in various ways to work toward the goal of winning the race. This involves eating certain foods, denying themselves certain pleasures, and putting a lot of time and energy toward the goal of becoming a champion. The compelling vision of victory is the driving force behind their self-restraint. Champion runners hold themselves accountable to a higher standard because of the forceful foresight of who they are and what they want to accomplish. That's what heavenly vision does for the believer; it raises the standards of accountability and motivates the highest of heavenly behaviors.

CALLING UP HIGHER *(Dano)*

When I personally recognized my calling to the nations and realized the need to train myself in praying and prophesying over places and national leaders, no one had to convince me to pray for an hour each day. My actions were not motivated by a sense of law, rule, or principle; instead, I was driven towards higher noble actions by a heavenly vision. Similarly, when I understood my calling to preach but had no invitations, I would diligently study the Bible and seek daily bread to share with others. I would spend hours crafting sermons based on spiritual revelations, even without a place to preach them. The discipline came from desire not from rules and regulations. My behaviors were shaped by a heavenly vision, not an earthly opportunity. I was not just studying in hopes of an opportunity to preach; I was seeing that this identity and destiny required a deep knowledge and hunger for the written word.

Anyone can hastily prepare themselves for a present opportunity, but a heavenly identity compels us to transform ourselves before earthly destiny opens its doors. Unfortunately, we often try to motivate people to Christian behaviors solely through principles and rules, neglecting the power of a compelling vision. We then accuse unrestrained believers of lacking love for God and proper behavior. Instead of lifting one another up, we tend to burden each other. A prophetic vision of the heavenly identity encoded in your name inspires virtuous behaviors, and encouragement infuses courage in you to live by a higher standard. The lower form of accountability serves as a boundary line that believers should not cross, but it fails to create a finish line that motivates and propels us towards manifesting our higher nature.

Every sin or lack of righteous performance can be traced to a vision problem. Lazy or sinful behavior is a sign that someone has forgotten or doesn't know who they are or what they are running for. In the heavenly view of accountability, when we see someone misbehaving, we don't just call them out for their sin, we call them up to their heavenly person. We say, "Hey, you are way too amazing to be acting like that. How does your current behavior line up with your heavenly calling? Remember who you are." In this way, we make it our goal to see one another as saints rather than sinners. We live expecting righteousness from one another and encouraging each other in our races. When someone stumbles or falls, we humbly remind them of who they are in Christ and help them stand and move forward.

UPGRADED EVANGELISM

Understanding the power in a name opens doors to evangelism. By using the power-in-a-name activations (such as meaning, associations, wordplay, and God-given new name), we've introduced you to how we can engage in dialogue with the Holy Spirit about any person's heavenly potential. The person God created one to be was embedded before time began. Even before someone accepts Christ or before a Christian understands their new creation, we can see glimpses of the glory of their heavenly identity residing in the power of their name.

We're not suggesting a belief system that everyone is already in a position of personal salvation. Each person comes to salvation through a personal work of faith in the heart and a resulting declaration with their mouth.[3]

What we are saying is that because God is intimately acquainted with every human from the time they were being formed in their mother's womb,[4] everyone who wears a name tag becomes a target for God's goodness! Whenever we hear or see a person's name, we have opportunity to engage in a conversation with the Holy Spirit about their potential identity in Christ.

Believers must choose to access the treasures of their heavenly identity in Christ Jesus. However, prophecy enables us to speak to a pre-Christian's heavenly potential in a way that leads them to repentance through the kindness of God.[5] By treating a person according to their treasure rather than their trash, we have the power to pull them into the kingdom of God rather than just scare the hell out of them. We are treasure hunters, not dumpster divers.

THE MINISTRY OF RECONCILIATION

This way of seeing pre-Christians is more than an evangelistic method, it is an assignment from Heaven for every believer. For evidence of this fact, let's go to Paul's message to the Corinthian church.

> Therefore, if anyone is in Christ, the new creation has come; the old has gone, the new is here! All this is from God, who reconciled us to himself through Christ and gave us the ministry of reconciliation: that God was reconciling the world to himself in Christ, not counting people's sins against them. And he has committed to us the message of reconciliation.
>
> 2 Corinthians 5:17-19

There it is. Our mission and ministry of reconciliation is defined as not treating sinners according to their sin or counting people's sins against them. How can we possibly do that? We look through the lens of heavenly identity. The ministry of reconciliation gives us the permission and the assignment to see the world and its people through the lens of their heavenly potential.

The power in a name is amplified through a heavenly lens, enabling us to see others as Christ does. Earthly perspectives are limited by our own observational skills and preconceived ideas, but a heavenly view liberates us to see pre-Christians in their reconciled state. Through the power revealed in their name, we can unlock their potential and bring Heaven to earth.

> "The power in a name is amplified through a heavenly lens which enables us to see others as Christ does."

HEAVENLY IDENTITY TOOLS

For an example of how you can apply heavenly identity within culture, consider when you sit down at a restaurant and the server introduces themselves. In addition to selecting your meal, you can also prepare a word of encouragement for them. While their team prepares an earthly meal for you, you can offer a heavenly morsel for them. When the server leaves the table, ask the Holy Spirit how He sees your server. Look up the meaning of their name and consider any of the power-in-a-name clues that come to mind as you ask. Be sure to honor your server's time by being brief, but when your server returns to your table, share something like, "You know, I couldn't help but notice how well your name fits you. Your name means... and I can see that God made you... I bet you are great at..." You don't have to lead them to salvation in that moment, but you can ignite their curiosity about how God sees them. You can use this technique in any scenario where you are transacting business with someone wearing a name tag.

PRAYING THE SOLUTION NOT THE PROBLEM

Heavenly identity is also a powerful prayer tool. When someone we love is behaving in a way that is troubling, we often pray about the problem. "Oh Lord," we cry, "help them not to do that anymore." It's not a bad prayer, but there is a more effective way to pray. Pray the power in their name. Let me show you an example using the name Michael. Because the name Michael means "Christ bearer, and the biblical archangel Michael is a warrior angel, a prayer for someone with this name might sound like, "Lord, you made Michael to be a Christ-bearer, a mighty one who defends Your causes and upholds Your standards like the angel of the Lord. He is a warrior of righteousness, and I call him into his place in Your kingdom..." In this way, we are praying from the heavenly solution not amplifying the complaints of the earthly problem.

Becoming aware of heavenly identity isn't just a way of seeing ourselves, but a way of partnering with Heaven in the redemption of all things and people. It gives us power tools to redefine culture and live from a heavenly viewpoint. Let us pray for the Holy Spirit to open our hearts to this heavenly view revealed in the power of a name.

CHAPTER REFLECTIONS

Is it more difficult for you to see yourself or others through a heavenly identity lens? How is embracing your own heavenly identity connected to your ability to see and value the identity of others?

_____
_____
_____
_____

Who is a person or place that you have had trouble seeing through a redemptive lens? What does the power of their name reveal about their heavenly potential? What steps of agreeing, aligning, and appropriating could you take towards that person or place in calling out their heavenly identity?

_____
_____
_____
_____

Are there any areas in which you have viewed God from an earthly rather than a heavenly view? Ask Holy Spirit to reveal them and replace them with His truth. Journal your discoveries below.

CHAPTER END NOTES

---

1. 2 Corinthians 5:17.

2. 1 Corinthians 9:25.

3. Romans 10:9-10.

4. Psalm 139:13-16, Jeremiah 1:5.

5. Romans 2:4.

Chapter 16

Name Above All Names

Throughout this book, we have discovered the treasure that is available to every person through their name. Each name is like a crown upon our heads that signifies our identity, authority, responsibility, and destiny. While every name given by God is powerful and unique, there is one name that surpasses them all. For centuries, people have been quoting and referencing a name that Heaven deems better and greater than all other names. Countless worship songs have been inspired and dedicated to this name. This name is so powerful and above all other names that it is known as the "name above all names." This title belongs exclusively to Jesus Christ.[1]

Why is Jesus' name considered the most elevated of all names? What is it about His name that gives Him unparalleled authority, not just in the present age but also in the future?[2] The answer can be seen in the prophetic meaning of His name.

SALVATION IN THE NAME

One of the greatest examples of the power in a name in the Bible is found in the meaning of the name of Jesus. As we mentioned in an earlier chapter, His name means *Jehovah is salvation* which represents who Jesus is as the Son of God and the Savior of the world. The mission and destiny of Jesus was deeply woven into His name when the angel Gabriel announced, "He will save His people from their sins." Do you see the connection? The meaning of Jesus' name relates both to who He is and what He came to do. Thus, an angel of the Lord appeared to Joseph in a dream and announced instructions for naming the child Mary was carrying along with a prophecy of His purpose: "She will bear a Son; and you shall call His name Jesus, for He will save His people from their sins."[3]

Not only was Jesus' name strategic for revealing His identity and purpose, but scripture also records that every person who believes in the name of Jesus will be saved. In other words, eternal life or death depends upon how we each personally relate to the name of Jesus. Consider the scriptures below for the weight of this truth.

> But as many as received Him, to them He gave the right to become children of God, to those who believe in His name....
>
> John 1:12

> These things I have written to you who believe in the name of the Son of God, so that you may know that you have eternal life.
>
> I John 5:13

The Savior of the world bears a name that carries the weight of His identity, purpose, and character. As we have learned, our names and our nature are inseparably linked. Jesus could not have been named anything else. His name could not have been *Abraham* because Jesus did not come to be the *father of many nations*. His identity and destiny were to be the Savior, and His name needed to fully express that. Thus, by believing and confessing His name—who He says He is and all that entails—any person can enter salvation. The importance of Jesus' name is consistently emphasized throughout scripture; it holds the power to save and transform lives.

As believers, we have access to the power and authority of the name of Jesus. We are called to pray and declare in His name, and we can trust that He hears and answers our prayers according to His will.[4] Our lives are to be lived in a way that reflects the identity and authority of Jesus. When we live in alignment with His name, we can experience the fullness of our own destiny and purpose.

THE ETERNAL NAME OF JESUS

The significance of Jesus' name is not limited to his earthly ministry. After His resurrection and ascension, Jesus continues to rule and reign with the power and authority that His name carries. In fact, the Bible tells us

> For this reason, also God highly exalted Him, and bestowed on Him the name which is above every name, so that at the name of Jesus every knee will bow, of those who are in heaven and on earth and under the earth, and that every tongue will confess that Jesus Christ is Lord, to the glory of God the Father.
>
> Philippians 2: 9-11

Jesus' name is exalted above every other name because it is the gateway to eternal life and to enjoying the fullness of God for ages to come. Believing in His name opens the door to this ultimate experience. Consider it this way: The name of Jesus is the key that unlocks the door to the benefits by which we will enjoy all the names and nature of God for eternity. People may experience certain benefits of God's names (e.g., Creator, Faithful,

Healer) on this side of Heaven, but unless a person confesses the name of Jesus as Lord, they will not enjoy the fullness of God beyond this temporal earthly life.

The name of Jesus surpasses every other name both now and forever because it is solely through Him that all creation and humanity find redemption. In the ages to come, we will always remember the reason and the means by which we reached eternity in the first place—Jesus.

Some say that there are many paths to God and Christianity is just one of the many. Scripture makes the distinction of Christ clear when it says, "Salvation is found in no one else, for there is no other name under heaven given to mankind by which we must be saved."[5] There is no other earthly name that can accomplish salvation for us—not Mohammad, Joseph Smith, Buddha, Confucius, Abraham, or the apostle Paul. No angel, no demon, no saint can do for mankind what believing in the name of Jesus can accomplish. He alone is the Savior of the world, and His name will forever be the Name Above All Names. It is His name alone that gives you access to the kingdom of God.

> "It is His name alone that gives you access to the kingdom of God."

BENEFITS OF THE NAME ABOVE ALL NAMES

With this understanding, let us look at a few passages that reference these and additional benefits that the name above all names brings to us.

1. **Forgiveness of sins** - "And you shall call His name Jesus, for He will save His people from their sins." (Matthew 1:21)

2. **Salvation** - "Salvation is found in no one else, for there is no

other name under heaven given to mankind by which we must be saved." (Acts 4:12)

3. **Deliverance from evil** - "And everyone who calls on the name of the Lord will be saved." (Acts 2:21)

4. **Healing** - "And these signs will accompany those who believe: In My name, they will drive out demons; they will speak in new tongues; they will pick up snakes with their hands; and when they drink deadly poison, it will not hurt them at all; they will place their hands on sick people, and they will get well." (Mark 16:17-18)

5. **Peace** - "And He will be called...Prince of Peace." (Isaiah 9:6)

6. **Partnership**- Whatever you ask in my name, this I will do, that the Father may be glorified in the Son. (John 14:13)

We can choose to bow our knees and believe in the name of Jesus while on this side of eternity, thereby, initiating the enjoyment of heavenly benefits while still here on earth. It's a name that carries power, hope, and victory.

Though one might choose not to acknowledge this name now, there is an actual, physical day coming when every tongue will confess that Jesus Christ is Lord.[6] If you have read this far, you probably know Jesus as your Savior already. If not, then will you choose Him now? Everyone who calls on the name of the Lord will be saved.[7] No one who calls on the name of the Lord will be left out of the benefits of this opportunity.

THE GRAND CANYON *(Dano)*

Even if you know Jesus as Savior, are you living under the full benefits of the name above all names? I compare it to my first trip with my wife to the Grand Canyon. Although I had visited the natural wonder as a child, she had not yet seen it. The canyon was along the route we were driving on a family road trip to the Midwest, so we stopped at the rim. We had driven for hours to get to this place, and now we stood at the edge of this massive hole in the earth. We looked deep into its depths, marveling at its width and breadth for about fifteen minutes. Then I turned to my wife and said, "Are you ready to go?"

She was flabbergasted. "You want to go already?"

"Well," I reasoned, "it's just a big hole. This is pretty much it. What did you want to do?"

"I want to ride a donkey down the trail or hike the rim. I want to experience the fullness of this place." I wasn't very sympathetic to her vision, and within minutes, we herded the kids back into our vehicle and left.

Years later, I had the chance to redeem that moment. My wife's parents were holding an anniversary celebration near the canyon, so we arranged for a second visit where we could spend more time. As we hiked just the first-quarter mile, I was shocked by how much the scenery changed. With each advance around the rim, we saw new colors, new shapes, and new discoveries. It was truly inspiring.

You see, I thought I had been to the Grand Canyon when I stood at the edge and took in what could be seen on that limited visit, but there was so much more to see and experience.

Many believers have stood on the edge of God's greatness in Christ Jesus and received Him as Savior. They think that in that one salvation experience of calling on the name of Jesus they have experienced the fullness of Christ this side of Heaven. But there is so much more to be experienced in Him who holds the name above all names.

While you are discovering the treasure map of identity and the road map of destiny hidden in your own name, make sure you are taking time to access all the treasures of the name that is above all. At the beginning of this journey into the power in a name, you probably did not realize all the benefits attached to who Christ made you to be. In the same way, many believers come to the door of salvation and then remain standing in the doorway, never entering the Kingdom benefits across the threshold. They assume that these treasures are reserved for after death. Their salvation in Christ is not in question, but is their experience with Christ like standing on the edge of the Grand Canyon not fully aware of the greatness of the place they are invited to explore?

In the same way that the authority, favor, and influence of your heavenly person are available to you now, the fullness of the risen, exalted, glorified Jesus is also available to you right now. You can access these treasures through the power of His name. Do you need healing, deliverance, or peace of mind? Don't wait. Through the same faith that you used to access salvation in Christ Jesus, you can experience all the benefits of His name.

Paul in his letter to the Ephesians said it this way, "Praise be to the God and Father of our Lord Jesus Christ, who has blessed us in the heavenly realms with every spiritual blessing in Christ."[8] Through the name above all names, you now have access to every blessing in the heavenly realms. Certainly, there are blessings and treasures reserved for the great beyond. But we have come to know and have believed that there are many more benefits presently within the power of His name than most believers are accessing.

> "Through the name above all names, you now have access to every blessing in the heavenly realms."

It is our prayer that this book has helped you find the treasure map of who Christ made you to be. We hope you have at least glimpsed some of the road map of your own destiny as revealed in the power in your own name. But, even greater, we hope and pray that you experience the full power and benefits of knowing, loving, and serving the name that is above all names, our Lord and Savior, Jesus Christ. To Him be the glory forever and ever.

CHAPTER REFLECTION

What does it mean to pray and declare in the name of Jesus? How can you live your life in a way that reflects the identity and authority of Jesus?

_____

_____

_____

_____

How can you be even more proactive in sharing the power and hope of Jesus' name with others?

_____

_____

_____

_____

What steps can you take to grow in your understanding and relationship with the Name Above All Names?

_____

_____

_____

_____

CHAPTER END NOTES

---

1. The name of Jesus in a few other languages around the world: Yeshua, Yesu, Isus, Исус, Jeesus, Xesús, Jezi, Yesus, Gesù, Ciise, Chúa Giêsu, uJesu.

2. Ephesians 1:21.

3. Matthew 1:21.

4. See John 14:13-14, 15:16, 16:23-25.

5. Acts 4:12.

6. Philippians 2:9-11.

7. Romans 10:13.

8. Ephesians 1:3.

About the Authors

Bethany Hicks is an international speaker, co-founder of Prophetic Company, and a best-selling author. Her works include *Own Your Assignment* and *The God Connection*. She is known as a strong communicator who releases passion and grace for people to embrace their world-changer identity.

As an author and international speaker with over thirty years of experience in prophetic ministry, Dan McCollam has trained thousands of individuals, church leaders, and organizations in recognizing and responding to the voice of God. Dan is co-founder of Prophetic Company, a ministry dedicated to activating prophetic voices globally.

Resources

HOST A PROPHETIC COMPANY IDENTITY CAMP

The Power in a Name is just one of the tools developed by Prophetic Company for unlocking your heavenly identity. For an immersive experience, consider attending or hosting a Prophetic Company Identity Camp where we use additional biblical and practical tools for further defining your new creation in Christ Jesus. For more information visit PropheticCompany.com.

OTHER BOOKS BY DAN AND BETHANY

The God Connection by Bethany Hicks

Own Your Assignment by Bethany Hicks

Love and Prophecy by Dan McCollam

The Good Fight: Prophetic Processing Manual by Dan McCollam

My Super Powers: Gift of Prophecy by Dan McCollam

PROPHETIC COMPANY ONLINE COURSES

Participate in various free and fee-based online self-paced courses at www.propheticcompanyacademy.thinkific.com.